Epochs of Church History

EDITED BY

PROFESSOR MANDELL CREIGHTON.

THE POPES AND THE HOHENSTAUFEN.

EPOCHS OF CHURCH HISTORY.

Edited by Professor MANDELL CREIGHTON.

Fcap. 8vo, price 2s. 6d. each.

THE ENGLISH CHURCH IN OTHER LANDS. By the Rev. H. W. TUCKER, M.A.

THE HISTORY OF THE REFORMATION IN ENGLAND. By the Rev. GEORGE G. PERRY, M.A.

THE CHURCH OF THE EARLY FATHERS. By ALFRED PLUMMER, D.D.

THE EVANGELICAL REVIVAL IN THE EIGHTEENTH CENTURY. By the Rev. J. H. OVERTON, M.A.

A HISTORY OF THE UNIVERSITY OF OXFORD. By the Hon. G. C. BRODRICK, D.C.L.

A HISTORY OF THE UNIVERSITY OF CAMBRIDGE. By J. BASS MULLINGER, M.A.

THE CHURCH AND THE ROMAN EMPIRE. By the Rev. A. CARR.

THE CHURCH AND THE PURITANS, 1570–1660. By HENRY OFFLEY WAKEMAN, M.A.

THE CHURCH AND THE EASTERN EMPIRE. By the Rev. H. F. TOZER, M.A.

HILDEBRAND AND HIS TIMES. By the Rev. W. R. W. STEPHENS, M.A.

THE ENGLISH CHURCH IN THE MIDDLE AGES. By the Rev. W. HUNT, M.A., Trinity College, Oxford.

THE POPES AND THE HOHENSTAUFEN. By UGO BALZANI.

IN PREPARATION.

THE ARIAN CONTROVERSY. By H. M. GWATKIN, M.A., Lecturer and late Fellow of St. John's College, Cambridge.

THE COUNTER-REFORMATION. By A. W. WARD.

THE GERMAN REFORMATION. By Prof. MANDELL CREIGHTON, M.A., D.C.L.

WYCLIF AND THE BEGINNINGS OF THE REFORMATION. By REGINALD LANE POOLE, M.A., Balliol College, Oxford.

CHURCH AND STATE IN MODERN TIMES.

THE REFORMATION IN ENGLAND.

THE WARS OF RELIGION.

THE CHURCH AND THE TEUTONS.

CHRISTIANITY AND ISLAM.

MONKS AND FRIARS.

LONDON: LONGMANS, GREEN, & CO.

THE POPES

AND

THE HOHENSTAUFEN.

BY

UGO BALZANI.

LONDON
LONGMANS, GREEN, AND CO.
1889.

Ballantyne Press
BALLANTYNE, HANSON AND CO.
EDINBURGH AND LONDON

PREFACE.

—⋆—

THE historical period traversed by this book is certainly
one of the most striking in the history of the Papacy
and the Empire, for their struggles far exceeded the
thoughts and aims of the combatants and hastened in
Europe a marvellous development of change and progress. The history of the relations between the Popes
and the Hohenstaufen is one which cannot be easily
kept within strict limits, but is apt to extend to that
of the whole of Europe and of much of the East. It
has been a difficult task to confine it within the small
space of these pages, nor could this have been done
without rigorously excluding everything which did
not bear directly on the relations of the Papacy with
the House of Suabia, and on those historical events
which exerted most influence over those relations,
especially in Italy, where the great drama was chiefly
acted. I have therefore tried to avoid all digressions
as much as possible, keeping distinctly before me the
object of the narrative, so as not to interrupt its
thread.

It also seemed to me that the nature of the work

demanded great moderation in generalising with regard to the facts stated in it, and I have therefore endeavoured that these facts should speak for themselves as clearly as possible, and should suggest those reflections which present themselves spontaneously to the reader who follows carefully the course of human events and meditates upon them. But in order to obtain this result, and not lead the reader to erroneous conclusions, the writer needs a very accurate knowledge of his facts, and a painstaking selection of those which have a vital importance for the narrative, and of those alone. This can only be secured by a long and minute study of the original historical sources; and hence, while making large use of the many valuable works which have preceded this little book, I have based my assertions throughout on original researches. In a very much larger and more detailed work on the same subject, which I hope at a not very distant day to publish in Italy, I propose to give the more complete result of these researches, and a scientific analysis of the facts and considerations which I have here put forward.

UGO BALZANI.

TICKTON LODGE, CLEVEDON, SOMERSET,
September 21, 1888.

CONTENTS.

—◆—

THE POPES AND THE HOHENSTAUFEN.

CHAPTER I.

(1125–1138.)

INTRODUCTORY.

THE great struggle for the investitures between the Papacy and the Empire had at last ended in the Concordat of Worms, and out of this struggle both the two great adversaries came exhausted, but neither of them entirely conqueror or wholly vanquished. The Papacy, though partially giving way in the question of the investitures, had gained ground, nevertheless, in matters of wider and more real importance. During the long period of the struggle, not only the men themselves had changed, but the very principles for which they were fighting were undergoing transformation, and the successors of Gregory VII. and Henry IV. moved in a different sphere of ideas from that which surrounded their great predecessors. The mere fact of having been able to hold out so firmly was a victory for the Papacy, and from the day in which Gregory had deposed Henry, and brought him to his knees at Canossa, all possibility had ceased of an imperial supremacy such as that exercised over the Popes by the Ottos and Henry III. Later, when the voice of Peter the Hermit, giving utterance to a cherished thought of the Roman pontiffs, aroused in the nations of Christendom a wild enthusiasm for the crusade declared by Urban II., the relations between Church and Empire underwent still further change. To the imperial conception of universal power it was a distinct blow that the whole of the Christian community should for the first time be aroused and directed towards a far-off and arduous war without the Empire's co-operation and guidance. Nor was this all. Other elements, either unknown before or unnoticed, began to appear on the scene of history, and while the long contest was reaching its conclusion a new era had risen above the horizon. Europe, freed from the dark barbarism in which preceding ages had enveloped her, found herself confronted by other problems, and was preparing for new enterprises.

When in 1125 the house of Franconia died out in the person of Henry V., Honorius II., who was then Pope, found himself very advantageously placed in regard to the Empire, and turned the opportunity to good account. On the 30th of August 1125, in the Diet of Mentz, the Duke of Saxony, Lothair of Supplinburg, was elected King of the Romans, but not without opposition, as another candidate for the throne was Frederick Duke of Suabia, who had many adherents, and was a near relation to the late Emperor. He was of the house of Weiblingen, and from one of their castles he and his family took the name of Hohenstaufen. Now, the Hohenstaufen would not acquiesce in the election of Lothair, and there was war in Germany. The Saxon Lothair attached himself to the Pope, and Honorius openly supported him, but profiting by his weakness, imposed the authority of the Papacy on the Empire to which he was aspiring, and obtained from the needy monarch humble demonstrations of reverence and willing submission. Thus the imperial authority was waning before the papal in the eyes of men, while the Empire itself, intended for Lothair, was weakened by the discords which were rending Germany. Bohemia had given Lothair a great deal of trouble, and the Hohenstaufen were still powerful against him. Frederick of Suabia had given up his pretensions in favour of his brother Conrad, who now contested the crown, and in December 1127 persuaded some of the princes to declare him king at Spires. He did not, however, meet with much favour, and especially the German clergy, whom Lothair flattered, were opposed to his usurping election. Conrad, seeing that he did not succeed in Germany, appealed to Italy, where, with the help of the Milanese archbishop, Anselm Pusterla, he was crowned with the iron crown at Milan, and in Tuscany put forward his pretensions to the inheritance of the Countess Matilda. These pretensions, and the traditions of his family, which were adverse to the Church, were in themselves enough to estrange from him Honorius, who remained a firm supporter of the pliant and legitimate Lothair. Conrad, excommunicated, and rendered for the time powerless, stayed on in Italy, protected rather than supported by isolated bishops or princes, and here and there by some municipality. It is a strange coinci-

dence that he was always favoured by the commune
of Milan, which was destined in time to become Italy's
strongest bulwark against the attacks of the house of
Suabia.

In the meantime Honorius died, and the election of
his successor gave rise to a schism in the Church.
Two cardinals were elected at the same time, both
Romans. One was Gregory, of the Papareschi, who
took the name of Innocent II., the other, Peter, of the
powerful family of the Pierleoni, assumed the name of
Anacletus II. Each had good reasons for asserting that
his election was canonical, so that the question remained
an open one, and the schism grew to such a height
that it was impossible either to suppress or to compose
it. Innocent and Anacletus both made great efforts to
draw over Lothair to their side, but he, taken up with
the discords in Germany, hesitated, and lost the opportunity of affirming his authority while the Papacy was
enfeebled by internal divisions. Other forces, however,
were making their influence felt in Europe, and they
served to balance, and sometimes to rule, that power
which hitherto was centred in the courts and councils
of kings. In a thousand different forms, and in almost
every direction, the universal conscience of the people
was awaking to a greater activity, and often declared
itself by the very voice of those who inspired it. A
wonderful man, Bernard of Clairvaux, whose fiery soul
felt all the mysterious fascination of his age, exercised
an extraordinary influence over European thought by
awakening in his contemporaries his own feelings. He
saw clearly how disastrous for the Church at this critical
moment any disunion must be, and, after a brief hesi-

tation, he threw himself resolutely into the contest. Espousing the cause of Innocent, he undertook his defence with that persevering, unflinching ardour peculiar to him; nor did he cease to support him till success crowned his efforts. First he obtained from France the recognition of Innocent, who had taken refuge there from Rome, where the party of Anacletus was the strongest. The example of France was followed by the king of England, and finally by Lothair, who in 1131 met Innocent at Liège, and was crowned there by him.

Thus the schism might have been healed, but in Italy the difficulties were more numerous, and the interests involved were complex and various. In North and Central Italy the communes, which were slowly growing during the struggle between the Church and Empire, had now reached a state of great prosperity. Feudalism, weakened, and even in many places destroyed, was losing ground before the invasion of popular government, and so was the temporal authority of the bishops, first raised by the Ottos, and favoured by other emperors. As no emperor had shown himself in Italy for a long time, the cities had taken advantage of this absence to increase their independence and free themselves from every fetter, without disputing the sovereignty of the Empire, but merely letting its rights drop out of use and paying little attention to its claims. They prospered wonderfully, and being favoured by the nature of the soil, by the qualities of the people, and by the freedom they enjoyed, they added power to riches. So while the Venetian, Genoese, and Pisan ships were wandering over distant seas in search of commerce and colonies, in Lombardy and Central Italy cities were rising everywhere rich in industries and culture, and Milan was foremost among the many Lombard towns, while Bologna became a famous intellectual centre, and Florence, fostered first by the Countess Matilda, and now rising in power, was unfolding the first pages of her glorious history, destined to prove so full of variety and attraction.

Except at Milan, the Antipope Anacletus had not met with much support in these parts of Italy, which were generally friendly to Innocent, and were, moreover, distracted by their own private interests, and by the quarrels and jealousies which were continually setting one city against another, and wasting much of their strength. But Anacletus, strongly entrenched in Rome, turned for support towards the South. There the Normans, who had formed a strong monarchy, regarded with suspicion alike by the Emperors of the East and of the West as a threatened obstacle to their ambitious views, showed themselves friendly or hostile to the Popes according to political exigencies. Very obsequious in speech, but cunning and resolute in purpose, they had frequent misunderstandings with the Popes, owing to the claims of the pontiff to suzerainty over the whole kingdom, and to his absolute possession of Benevento and some other places. Roger I. shrewdly made use of the schism, and protected Anacletus, who was both the nearer and the weaker, receiving in exchange the recognition of the royal title he had assumed, the investiture of his kingdom, his claims to which were thus sanctioned, and other exemptions and privileges, which, though only conceded to him by an Antipope, were to be later confirmed and recognised. The power of Roger, strengthened by these concessions, became threatening both for the interests of the Papacy and for those of the Empire, so that Lothair decided to visit Italy notwithstanding his difficulties and wars in Germany. He met with some opposition, not sufficient to stop him, but showing the spirit of the times which were approaching. On the plains of Roncaglia, near Piacenza, he and Innocent II. met and marched on together to Rome. There Lothair was received without hostilities, but was obliged, contrary to custom, to receive the imperial crown in the Lateran, because Anacletus and the Pierleoni faction held the right bank of the Tiber and were masters of St. Peter's.

On this occasion the Pope and the Emperor confirmed once more without substantial alterations the conditions of the treaty of Worms with regard to the investitures, but as for the claims which both put forward to the inheritance of the Countess Matilda, while the Pope yielded them for life and by feudal investiture to Lothair, he exacted at the same time a recognition of his rights over them and of his sovereignty. This was a great point gained, and the Popes were to make use of it later. A picture representing Lothair at the Pope's feet in the act of receiving the imperial crown was placed in the Lateran to commemorate this event, and under it were inscribed two lines expressing very clearly the idea of the Roman court, and destined later to excite discussions and discontent in Germany. The lines ran thus :—

"Rex stetit ante fores iurans prius urbis honores,
    Post homo fit Papæ, sumit quo dante coronam."

Without attempting anything against Anacletus,
who remained master of Rome, or against Roger of
Sicily, Lothair soon returned to Germany, where
things took a rapid turn in his favour, and even the
Hohenstaufen submitted themselves to him. Grown
more powerful in consequence, and invoked by the
Pope and St. Bernard, Lothair made a second descent
into Italy in 1136. Here and there in the cities,
growing more and more in vigour and independence,
he met with opposition, which he baffled partly by
force, partly by prudence. St. Bernard, in the meantime, in his persevering apostolate against the schism,
had succeeded in separating Milan from the faction
of Anacletus. Innocent, finding his position in Rome
untenable, had taken refuge at Pisa, where he held
a council attended by St. Bernard, and thence went
to meet Lothair at Bologna. Then, instead of going
to Rome, the Pope and Emperor decided to proceed to the South against Roger of Sicily, and
the expedition proved successful. Lothair and his
Germans, with the assistance on the sea-side of the
Genoese and Pisan ships, marched victoriously across
Italy, ravaging everywhere as they passed, and taking
Capua, Salerno, and Bari, while Innocent entered and
regained possession of Benevento. But shortly afterwards, in a question touching the Abbey of Monte-
cassino and the Duchy of Apulia, the same reasons and
claims which created dissensions between the Normans
and the Popes, aggravated by the inevitable antagonism of papal and imperial authority, began to bring

about disagreement between Innocent and Lothair, which, however, had no serious or lengthened consequences. Lothair, suffering from age and infirmities, thought of returning home. In the monastery of Farfa, in Sabina, he separated from the Pope and started for Germany, but died on the journey in the Tyrol, the 3rd of December 1137. His death cleared the way to the throne for Conrad of Hohenstaufen, who was elected King of the Romans on the 7th of March 1138, and on the 13th of the same month was crowned at Aix-la-Chapelle.

The Roman faction of the Pierleoni had lost ground through the defeat of Roger, and the Frangipani brought back Innocent to Rome. He was now universally recognised as Pope, and the eloquence of St. Bernard was successful in detaching from Anacletus some of his staunchest and most influential supporters, and even in shaking Roger of Sicily, who, however, did not yield to the extent of closing a schism advantageous to himself. The deserted Antipope died shortly afterwards. A new Antipope arose under the name of Victor IV., but before long St. Bernard brought him a penitent to the feet of Innocent, and the schism was at an end. In a Lateran Council the acts of Anacletus were solemnly annulled, and a sentence of excommunication went forth against Roger, who had again got the upper hand, had reoccupied Apulia, and invaded the possessions of the Church. Innocent, not contenting himself with spiritual weapons, very imprudently made war upon him in person and entered his kingdom, but was soon surrounded and taken prisoner. The wily Norman was profuse in demonstrations of reverence and devotion towards his prisoner, and thus obtained from him the investiture of the kingdom and the full confirmation of all that Anacletus had given up to him.   After this reconciliation with Roger, Innocent returned, humbled and frustrated, to Rome, where fresh storms were gathering on the horizon.

CHAPTER II.

(1138–1154.)

EUGENIUS III. AND CONRAD OF HOHENSTAUFEN—
ELECTION OF FREDERICK I.

THE great municipal movement which spread rapidly
in Italy extended even to Rome, where perhaps a
certain autonomy in civic government had never quite
ceased, more or less marked according to the turn of
events. It may be said that the life of the Roman
municipality never died out, but through all the Middle
Ages oscillated like the light of a lamp trembling
in the wind, now flaring up, now to all appearance
quenched. Certainly, while elsewhere the commune
developed and grew strong, in Rome it always met
with special hindrances. Rome, situated in the centre
of a deserted plain, unfavourable to agriculture or
commerce, was wanting in all those material resources
which seconded the efforts of other cities. The middle-
class had few means of increasing or strengthening
their position, and had against them the powerful and
quarrelsome nobles, who often divided the people into
factions, and made use of these divisions to weaken
them. The Papacy and the Empire, with their rights

and claims of sovereignty, circumscribed the civic liberties, and through their political universality absorbed
the public life of the city, rendering it impossible
for it to expand.   Besides, Rome was a hindrance to
herself.   Weighed down by her great name, she lost
herself in the pursuit of brilliant dreams, and strove
to reacquire a position which she could no longer
reach.   She thus lost ground instead of gaining it,
and, in truth, all her political life was impoverished by
the halo which surrounded her name.

Notwithstanding this, at the time of which I am
speaking, a new and not inglorious period was opening
in her history, and the commune, through a better
organisation of its forces, was able in the last days of
Innocent II. to affirm its independence with greater
confidence.   Disappointed by Innocent, who, instead
of destroying their rival Tivoli, conquered by their
arms, made her subject to himself, the Romans rose,
and throwing off the papal yoke, formed themselves
into a free republic.   It was the year 1143.   Old
names, never entirely forgotten, were revived ; the
Capitol was restored, the name of senator renewed,
—memories and illusions which had been lovingly
cherished through ages of fallen greatness.   The great
nobles, almost always hostile to any attempt to develop
the Roman commune, this time for a moment did
not oppose it, while it was especially favoured by a
lesser nobility, who, issuing in a certain measure from
the people, and bound to it, succeeded in holding the
government of the city with a sufficiently firm hand,
in as far as the times, full of hindrances and rapid
changes, would permit.

Innocent II., overcome by the revolution and worn out, died shortly afterwards in September 1143; nor could Celestin II., who was Pope after him for only a few months, do anything towards subduing the Romans. His successor, Lucius II., was even more unfortunate. First he tried to oppose Roger of Sicily, refusing to confirm Innocent II.'s concessions; but Roger threw a band of soldiers into the Campagna, who ravaged it as far as Ferentino, and occupied Terracina. The Romans meanwhile took the opportunity of abolishing the office of prefect, whose authority was exercised on the Pope's behalf, and renewed in his place the ancient dignity of patrician, with powers held from themselves. Having raised Giordano Pierleoni to this position, they intimated to the Pope to hand over to him all the royalties within and without the city. After having vainly invoked the aid of Conrad of Hohenstaufen, whose troubles at home prevented his giving any heed, Lucius II. attempted to seize the Capitol by force, but was repulsed. He died the 15th of February 1145, some say from a wound inflicted by a stone during the unsuccessful assault on the Capitol.

To him succeeded Bernard, abbot of the monastery of St. Anastasius at the Three Fountains near the Ostian Basilica, a disciple of St. Bernard, who at first seemed alarmed at the election, expecting from the new Pope less aptitude for government than was afterwards shown by him. He took the name of Eugenius III. He reached the papacy in very stormy times, and had to commence by flight in order not to bow to the Roman senate, which threatened forcibly to prevent his consecration unless he would recognise the independence of the city. First he took refuge in the monastery of Farfa, where he was consecrated the 4th of March 1145, then went to reside at Viterbo, as it was impossible to return to Rome, where the republican constitution was daily being more and more firmly organised.

But these republican and reforming tendencies did not attack the idea of the Empire and Papacy, which in the mind of all Christendom was inseparable from the idea of human society. Rome only desired to shake herself free from the immediate rule of the Pope by creating a separate and popular government, and, in her confused love for all that was ancient, was disposed to amalgamate with the republic, and make again her very own that Empire which had now become essentially German, and retained nothing Roman but its name and its claims on a dominion over the city.

Characteristic of this is a letter which the Romans sent, a little later, to Conrad III., inviting him to Rome to receive from them the imperial crown, and take up his residence in the ancient metropolis of the world, whence he could far better rule over Italy and Germany. But the insuperable difficulties in the way of any such supremacy for them regarding the Empire as much as the Papacy soon showed themselves. Conrad did not even reply to the request of the Romans, and already the Pope had found support in the jealousies aroused by the new republic. Not satisfied with depriving the Pope of every dominion within the city, the Romans began now to attempt to do the same in the surrounding country, and to extend their own power. This attempt met with prompt resistance. The neighbouring cities, hated by Rome and hostile to her, and the great Roman nobles, fearing for their possessions in the Campagna, which were the sources of their power, united themselves with the Pope against Rome. The city had soon to yield, to receive the Pope within her walls, abolish the patrician, restore the prefect, recognise again the sovereignty of the Church, and promise to pay her tribute. The Pope celebrated the Christmas of 1146 with all solemnity in Rome, but he was not strong enough to govern the city. The new republican order remained, and the authority of the senate continued as before. In reality, rather than a peace between subjects and sovereign, a truce had been concluded between two contending parties; nor did the truce last long. Very soon fresh grounds for disagreement obliged Eugenius to leave Rome a second time, and the Romans were still free.

Henceforth it was clear that the Pope could not return to Rome with any prospect of security without the assistance of King Conrad, and Eugenius reiterated his prayers that he should descend into Italy, restore order, and receive the imperial crown. The Lombard cities, arrogant, forgetful of their subjection to the Empire, and in continual broils among themselves, Rome in rebellion, the ever-increasing and menacing power of Roger of Sicily, all these were reasons for his coming. But Conrad delayed without refusing. He had too many anxieties in Germany to be able to leave it easily and throw himself into such an enterprise, and perhaps he secretly was not ill pleased at the dissensions between the Pope and the Romans. These even increased instead of diminishing, encouraged as they were by Arnold of Brescia, who was in Rome at this time, and the soul of the new republic.

That spirit of inquiry which with Anselm of Aosta had started from the standpoint of Faith to seek the reason of things, was now threading the opposite path with Abelard, working out dangerous problems, subtle, inquisitive, almost petulant, starting from Reason to scrutinise the mysteries of Faith. And Arnold, differing from his master Abelard in greater force of character, less speculative and more inclined to action, was like him in his impatience with what appeared to him false, and in his pugnacity in trying to overthrow it. His adversaries say that he loved popularity, and perhaps, man of the people as he was, he did love it, but his heart burnt with an apostolic zeal which left him no rest. He was pious, austere, eloquent; persecutions, exile, his wandering life, all added fuel to the flame and energy to his character. In Lombardy first he had aroused enthusiasm, preaching against the immorality and riches of the clergy; he was persecuted by Maifred, bishop of Brescia, and condemned by the Church, was obliged to go into exile, and took refuge in France towards the end of 1139. The following year this ardent man appeared at the famous Council of Sens by the side of Abelard, true and steadfast against St. Bernard, his master's great enemy, and henceforth inexorably his own. And when Abelard gave way before the terrible monk, Arnold held out, and at St. Geneviève, where years before he had listened to his master's teaching, he undertook to lecture, and added perhaps on his own account violent invectives against the corrupt Church and her principal rulers. St. Bernard attacked him. They were two apostles, unspotted and tenacious, armed for the combat with equal ardour but unequal weapons. Bernard had on his side the spirit of his times, and was the stronger. Arnold was obliged to leave France, and withdrew to Zurich, where he gained followers, but, persecuted there also, he took refuge under the protection of a Cardinal Guido, who was then legate in Germany. With him he returned to Italy, and at Viterbo saw Eugenius III., who absolved him on condition that he should do penance as a pilgrim at the Roman shrines, and Arnold accepted the condition, if we may trust a well-informed contemporary, John of Salisbury, the only one who reports this circumstance. But soon after Arnold reappears the same man as before, spreading his teaching of reform and freedom in Rome. To the republican movement of Lombardy, to the traditions of the *Pataria*, which had crept in among the common people of his native Brescia, and now betrayed an heretical tendency, to the philosophical movement in Paris, where Arnold had absorbed the teachings of Abelard, to all these influences was added a literary awakening which led men's intellects towards the pure sources of Latin writers, and was an early prelude of the Renaissance, arousing in all hearts the love and the memory of classic lore. As he gazed from the restored Capitol down on the broken columns of the Forum, how could he escape the silent charm of those scattered ruins; and surrounded as he was by sacred memories of the primitive Church, her humility and holy poverty, how could he help inveighing against the worldliness and riches of the Church of his day? So the thunders of his voice aroused the Romans, who, eager for novelty, listened to him gladly, and gave him a large share in the councils and the government of their city, where, among other things, he helped to reorganise, under the old name of *equestrian order*, that militia composed of the lesser nobles and of the more conspicuous families of the people which formed the sinews of the army in the free republics of Lombardy.

In the meantime, serious events were agitating Christendom, and for a moment took off the attention of Eugenius III. from Rome. The first Crusade had not broken the power of the Mussulman, and from the Eastern Christians came continual and persistent entreaties for help, and accounts of injuries suffered and dangers menaced. The Pope turned to the French for a new crusade, and King Louis VII. declared his readiness to undertake it. Eugenius then confided to St. Bernard the mission of proclaiming the holy war among the nations. His preaching aroused the greatest enthusiasm in all classes. The churches were too small to contain his hearers, and he was obliged to preach in the open air to the crowds who flocked to take the cross from the hands of this inspired man speaking in the name of God. From France Bernard passed into Germany, and at Mentz, Frankfort, and Spires, wherever he went, the excitement was the same. Conrad III. received the apostle of the cross with due honour, but, on the plea that the affairs of his kingdom would not allow of it, showed unwillingness to take part in the enterprise.

Popular feeling, however, was strong, and a more than usually eloquent sermon of St. Bernard's seemed to overcome his hesitation, so that, much moved and in tears, he interrupted the Saint in order to offer himself to God and take up the cross. Bernard regarded this as a miracle worked by God, nay, as he called it, the miracle of miracles; but in his apostolic zeal he had far exceeded the prudent wishes of the Pope. Eugenius would have preferred that Conrad should have remained in Europe to look after Germany and to be free to come into Italy, receive the imperial crown, and restore papal authority in Rome. But it was not for the Pope to make difficulties in such a case. When Conrad had put the affairs of the kingdom into some sort of order, he had his youthful son Henry proclaimed king, and left him ruler of the state under a regency. Together with Conrad, a nephew of his had taken the cross, Frederick, son of Frederick of Suabia, a young man of brilliant promise, who was to acquire his first reputation as a warrior in the East, and, after having filled Europe with his name, was to return there later to end a life full of glorious vicissitudes.

While this crusading excitement was at its height, Eugenius III. had gone to France in March 1147, and had blessed its king before his departure. There the Pope resided for about a year, and for some time he also went to Germany, attending principally to the ecclesiastical affairs of those countries, and in the absence of the sovereigns trying to gain power and adherents for the Church. He was received with great honour at Paris and Triers, and held a solemn council at Rheims. But he did not gain all the influence he expected, and left France just as the first mournful tidings came of the Crusaders' misfortunes in arms. Amidst the general discouragement the Church and the Pope lost ground, whereas he had hoped that this crusade should increase their dignity and power among the nations. Eugenius, on returning to Italy, found himself as before in difficulties with regard to Rome, and saw little prospect of assistance. He could not turn to Germany, as there the internal discords were raging more fiercely than ever; his journey had somewhat diminished his influence with the clergy there, and the archbishops of Cologne and Mentz were his enemies. Besides, Conrad's absence deprived the Germans of every opportunity of interfering in Italian affairs. From the Italian republics there was no support to be expected, or if any, of a most inefficient description. Meanwhile, Arnold of Brescia in republican Rome continued fierce and implacable, spreading his doctrines, which were subversive of the discipline and temporal constitution of the Church, and here and there heterodox in doctrine.

As soon as Eugenius reached Lombardy, he felt the necessity of making a stand against such attacks, and from Brescia herself he hurled forth anathemas against the daring Brescian innovator. This latter, however, did not yield, but continued with ever-increasing ardour to speak against the evils of the Papal Court to the Romans, who clung ever the more to him and promised to defend him against every enemy. Eugenius came on to Pisa, and having gained over that town to his cause, advanced towards Rome as far as

Tusculum. Determined to re-enter the city, and seeing no other means, he collected an army at a great
cost, thereby scandalising St. Bernard and another
eminent ecclesiastic, Gerohus of Reichersberg, from
both of whom he received letters full of bitter re-
proaches. With these soldiers, and assisted by the
greater Roman nobles, unchangingly hostile to the
republic, and by Roger of Sicily, who was approaching
the Church again with a view to obtaining definitely
the concessions he wanted, Eugenius threatened Rome.
The city, hard pressed, was obliged to agree to let him
enter once more in November 1149. But the senate
would on no account allow Arnold to be exiled from
Rome, and the republic remained with its prophet
respected and unharmed in spite of the Pope, who,
notwithstanding his armed bands, re-entered the town
rather as a guest than as a master.

It is easy to understand how Eugenius could not
this time either remain long in Rome. In June 1150
he retired to Albano, then to Anagni and Ceprano,
where he met Roger of Sicily, and entered into long
negotiations with him touching the questions per-
petually pending between the courts of Rome and
Sicily. The investiture of the kingdom and the concessions implying a more or less formal renunciation
of papal pretensions in Apulia were the knot which
nothing availed to untie, and which prevented any
lasting understanding; so that not even from Roger
could any efficient assistance be reckoned upon for the
subjugation of Rome and the expulsion of Arnold.

But in this interval Conrad III. had returned from
the Crusade at a fortunate moment for Germany, as the

dissensions had increased during his absence, and only a boy's hand was holding the reins of state. The old and unhealed feud between the Welf and the Weiblingen families broke out worse than ever, and a number of important questions in Poland and elsewhere demanded Conrad's immediate attention. But he also recognised the urgency of his presence in Italy, where the various republics were growing oblivious of the ties which should bind them to Germany, and where it still remained for him to assume the Roman crown of empire. Above all, he was suspicious of King Roger, who, master of the whole south of Italy, had widely extended his power by sea and land, and by successful naval expeditions against Greece and the coast of Africa had possessed himself of Tripoli and Tunis, while the crusading forces were wasting themselves in fruitless efforts against the Mussulman in the Holy Land.

The republican senate of Rome and the Pope both had recourse to Conrad, each offering him the crown, of which both thought themselves the rightful dispensers. The letter of the Romans, to which we have already alluded, perhaps written or inspired by Arnold of Brescia, exhorted the King to come and affirm once more the imperial supremacy over the Pope, insinuating at the same time that Eugenius was unfriendly to him and in secret alliance with Roger. The Pope, on the other hand, accused the Romans of wanting to elect an emperor of their own without regard to the rights of the German king. Conrad paid little heed to the Romans and entered into negotiations with the Pope, which dragged on slowly, and were repeatedly inter-

rupted and then taken up again. The principal ground
for delay was the still unsettled state of Germany,
consequent specially on the revolt of Henry the Lion,
Duke of Saxony, celebrated for the crusade he had
undertaken against the heathen Slavs and for his victories over them. Moreover, there contributed other
causes of delay: the then poor health of Conrad, the
death of his son, the thirteen-year old King Henry,
which added to the fears and agitations of Germany,
and perhaps also a certain almost instinctive feeling of
suspicion between the German and Papal courts. One
would have said that some adverse fate held Conrad
back from Italy, but at length everything seemed
settled, and the expedition into Italy decided on.
After bending the pride of the Lombard cities, he was
to assume the imperial crown, put down the Roman
rebellion, and, with Constantinople and Venice as allies,
destroy the kingdom of Sicily. The 11th of June
1151, at the Diet of Regensburg he publicly announced
the undertaking, and it was favourably received by
many of the princes. In September he repeated the
announcement at the Diet of Würzburg, and agreed
with his barons to make the expedition in the following year, thinking in the meantime to arrange matters
in Germany and put an end to the revolt of Henry the
Lion. Meanwhile he had sent his ambassadors to
Constantinople and to the Pope, the first to strengthen
the alliance against Roger, the others to facilitate the
journey to Italy and come to an understanding with
the Pontiff, who received them with the greatest cor-
diality. But the crown of the Empire was not destined for Conrad, and on the 15th of February 1152

he died at Bamberg after fourteen years' reign. He left an only son, Frederick, a boy of eight, but in his last moments, reflecting on the disturbed state of Germany and of the Empire, he prudently recommended to the electors as his successor his nephew Frederick of Hohenstaufen, Duke of Suabia.

The 4th of March 1152 Frederick was elected king at Frankfort, and men's minds turned anxiously to him, full of hope that he might be able to re-establish order in the thoroughly disorganised realm. During the reign of Conrad Germany had passed through endless internal struggles in a period of painful growth, and the arduous times had hindered and diminished the efficacy of that sovereign's valuable qualities. He had been obliged to undertake too many things, and consequently had hardly been able to complete any. It was for his successor to concentrate the scattered forces, combine and order them for one common object, give Germany quiet within and authority without by raising afresh the dignity of the Roman Germanic Empire, now so enfeebled as to seem destined to perish for want of vitality, unless some one should be found to restore it once more to the glorious days of Charlemagne and the first Otto. And indeed the spirit of those great men animated the youthful ambition of Frederick, who ascended the throne with his imagination full of their greatness, and his heart burning to imitate them. From his father he inherited the Ghibelline blood of the Hohenstaufen, through his mother he was related to the family of the Guelphs, thus blending in his person the two rival races, as if in him were at last to be quenched the animosities which for so long had steeped Germany in blood. He was scarcely thirty, of middle stature, of pleasing and dignified appearance; his teeth were white, his mouth full and smiling; he had blue eyes, a fresh colour, red hair and beard, whence the famous name of Barbarossa given to him by the Italians. Skilled in arms, careless of fatigue or danger, he had gained a high reputation in the East and in his own country as a valiant and experienced leader. Resolute, born to command, discriminating, he understood ruling men, and, when necessary, flattering them. He was severe and often ferocious against such opposition as he could break down by force or in the impetus of war, and showed his ferocity sometimes calculatingly, sometimes in real anger, but never was coldly or uselessly cruel. Longing for glory, ambitious, haughty and tenacious, but neither so haughty nor so tenacious as not to know how to yield when necessary, and prosecute his ends by other means. His culture was not great, but his intelligence was quick, and he enjoyed the conversation of learned men; and though he spoke Latin with difficulty, he read it with pleasure, especially histories telling of the grandeur and glory of that empire which he wished to restore. For on him also the revival of classic culture exercised its wonted fascination, and around him gathered the Italian jurists who were reviving the study of Roman imperial law, and saw in him the restored image of the ancient Empire. Vain evocation! The first Frederick of Hohenstaufen was in truth a German emperor, nor perhaps did any sovereign ever represent a more perfect type of the virtues and failings of Teutonic genius.

As soon as he had assumed the crown at Aix-la-Chapelle on the 9th of March 1152, Frederick sent into Italy as ambassadors Illinus, archbishop-elect of Triers, and Eberard, bishop of Bamberg. After that he immediately turned his attention to the affairs of Germany, first on the Rhine and then in Saxony, where there was special need of his care. At Merserburch he held a diet to decide a question pending between two Danish princes, Sweyn and Cnut, both pretenders to the throne of Denmark. Sweyn received the royal title, and did liege homage to Frederick. A more difficult question arose immediately afterwards in Saxony which brought Frederick into contact with the Roman Church. People's minds were divided regarding the election of the archbishop of Magdeburg, part of the votes being given to Gerard, provost of the Magdeburg diocese, part to the dean of the same church. When the matter was brought before the King, he induced those who supported the dean to give their votes to a third, the bishop Wichmann, and without further delay recognised him and invested him with the royalties. He thus introduced by implication a favourable interpretation of the rights which the Concordat of Worms had given him. Then he started for Bavaria, where he found the ambassadors sent by him into Italy, who were bringing him good accounts of their reception. In fact, Eugenius III. had written immediately from Segni to Frederick, congratulating him on his election, and expressing a hope that he would proceed to Rome to fulfil the promise made by Conrad; he also announced that he would soon send an embassy. And a few months later, in writing to

Vibald, abbot of Corvey, Eugenius returned to the subject which most nearly touched him, telling of the changes which the heretical Arnold was planning in Rome without the knowledge of the nobles and leading men of the city, and telling also of the two thousand people who were conspiring shortly to elect a hundred senators for life, and two consuls, one of whom they would have proclaimed emperor. He concluded the letter by asking the abbot to confide these matters in secret to Frederick.

Notwithstanding his pressing need and desire to gain over the new king, Eugenius did not show any disposition to yield in the matter of Magdeburg, and protested that Frederick had exceeded his powers, and that the canon law did not recognise the translation of Wichmann made in that way. But Frederick stood firm, and the question was still unsettled when Eugenius III. died at Tivoli on the 8th of July 1153, after having made another short stay in Rome. His successor, Anastasius IV., was obliged to yield to the strong will of Frederick and grant the pallium to Wichmann. Meanwhile Frederick was giving all his attention to establishing order in Germany, and initiated the decision regarding the contested duchy of Bavaria in favour of the Saxon Henry the Lion, a powerful prince, whom he loved and wished to conciliate with the Empire. He wanted him with him in Italy, whither he was drawn by the presentiment of great enterprises, the imperial crown, the exhortations of the exiled barons of Apulia conspiring against the Sicilian king, and the invitations of many Italian cities, who hoped for assistance from him against powerful

neighbours.   Nor were all these strong attractions
without avail.   Towards the October of 1154 Frederick left by way of the Tyrol for Italy, reached Verona,
and in November was encamped near Piacenza on the
plains of Roncaglia, where, according to custom, he held
his first Italian diet.   A few days later, on the 3rd of
December 1154, Anastasius IV. died in Rome.   With
his successor began a new era, which binds together
inextricably until the end the history of the house of
Suabia and of the Papacy.

CHAPTER III.

(1154-1155.)

HADRIAN IV. AND ROME—CORONATION OF FREDERICK I.

THE new Pope was Hadrian IV. He was born in England at St. Albans of poor parents, and his name was Nicholas Breakspear. He left when a youth his native land, wandered about France in search of instruction, and after studying some time at Arles, entered the monastery of St. Rufus near Valence, and there took the monastic garb. His quick intelligence, his piety, his zeal, rapidly gained him the consideration of the brethren, who, after first making him prior, by common consent raised him to the dignity of abbot. Business connected with the monastery called him to Rome during the pontificate of Eugenius III., who, instead of restoring him to his abbey, made him cardinal bishop of Albano, and appointed him to the Norwegian missions. In preaching the gospel to the heathen in those remote regions, and in organising the constitution of a church there, he gained a high reputation. On the death of Anastasius the cardinals unanimously turned to him, who had only just returned from

his successful apostolate, and on the 4th of December
1154 they elected him Pope.

He had strong shoulders for the burden which he
was taking up.   Conscious of assuming a lofty office
in an hour of special difficulty, full of zeal for the
Church's honour, piety in him was combined with a
talent for public affairs bordering on astuteness, and
the gentleness of his manners with a strong and resolute character.   Very soon an opportunity arose for
proving his firmness.   In Rome the discontent with
the Popes continued, and the new election could not
certainly meet with the approbation of the Romans or
cool their party spirit, since they regarded this stranger
as intent on increasing the papal rule, and, having lived
long in France, probably imbued with St. Bernard's
hatred of the doctrines of Arnold.   This latter, despis-
ing Hadrian's prohibition, had remained in Rome under
the protection of the senate, and openly preached
against the new Pope and his cardinals.   Excitement
was leading men to violence.   One day, while Guido,
the cardinal of St. Pudenziana, was going to the Pope,
he was attacked and wounded by a group of Arnold's
followers.   The Pope answered this mad violence by
placing the city under an interdict, and declaring that
he would maintain it until Arnold was driven from
Rome.   This new and unexpected event terrified the
people.   In vain they beseeched the Pope to retract
the heavy sentence ; Hadrian was immovable.   Easter
was approaching and Passion Week had already begun, yet the altars of the sacred city were prayerless
and closed to the faithful.   Under the influence of
religious terror the Romans yielded, and Arnold was

abandoned and driven forth. Wandering over the Campagna, he fell into the hands of papal soldiers who were looking for him, but was liberated by certain friendly barons, and took refuge in a castle of theirs on the confines of Tuscia. The city was absolved and Hadrian triumphed. For the first time since his election he issued from the Leonine city, traversed Rome in great pomp, and celebrated Easter in the Lateran.

While matters were turning out thus in Rome, there flared up again the old causes of discontent between the Curia and the King of Sicily, William I., who had succeeded shortly before to Roger. The new king, finding himself in troubled waters in the beginning of his reign, between rebels within and the external hostilities of the two Empires, thought he would try if he could gain the friendship of the Pope and separate him from Frederick. On Hadrian's election he sent ambassadors to treat peace with him, but they could come to no understanding. Later, towards the March of 1155, William having passed over from Sicily to Salerno, the Pope, perhaps alarmed at his coming nearer, sent Henry, cardinal of Saints Nereo and Achilleo, with apostolic letters. But since these bore on their front the ambiguous title of *Lord* instead of *King* of Sicily, William refused to receive the cardinal, which greatly disturbed the Pope and the whole Curia. Thus, instead of being appeased, the King was embittered the more in his relations with the Church, and sent against the territory of St. Peter his chancellor Ascontinus, who attempted the siege of Benevento, and overrunning the Campagna, set fire to several places,

among which Ceprano and Bauco. The Pope had to
content himself with excommunicating William and
looking for help from the North.

Hadrian had speedily resumed the negotiations for
the coronation of Frederick, interrupted by the deaths
of the preceding Popes, and the terms of alliance between the Pope and the future emperor, now settled in
general, were based on the subjugation of the Roman
republic and of the King of Sicily. Meanwhile
Frederick, from the first days that he had arrived in
Lombardy, felt that he was standing on a volcano, and
could not hope for dominion in Italy unless he first
crushed the strength of the republics which surrounded
him, proud of their prosperity, and, notwithstanding
their internal discords, little awed by the majesty of
the Empire. At Roncaglia he had appeared as judge
and pacificator between the various republics, and
especially between Pavia and Milan; but already this
latter, more powerful than any other Lombard city, was
a thorn in his side which it behoved him to remove.
Shortly he began openly to declare himself hostile to
Milan, either really angry or pretending to be so, because
his army had been guided awrong by the Milanese
in their own territory. He entered Rosate, a strong
castle of the Milanese, and driving out the inhabitants,
set fire to it, and in the same way burnt the castles of
Trecate and Galliate. In the cause of the Empire in
Italy was rooted the cause of feudalism, the power of
which was waning before the emancipation of the
communes. The city of Asti and the strong castle of
Chieri would no longer remain subject to the Marquis
of Monferrato, on whose instigation Frederick took Asti

and Chieri, and destroyed them by fire and sword.
Against Milan herself the King did not venture. She
was too powerful and too well provisioned, and Frederick
in attacking her would have run the risk of weakening his forces at the very beginning of his undertaking, or at least of delaying too long his coronation at
Rome. He thought it wiser to subdue some other town
friendly to Milan, and thus diminish her resources and
spread through Lombardy a wholesome terror of his
arms and of his name. Incited thereto by Pavia, he
turned against Tortona, desiring her to separate from
and break off all friendship with Milan, but Tortona
nobly refused. Frederick surrounded her, thinking to
conclude the siege quickly, but he met with a desperate
resistance, the presage of future struggles. Attacked
furiously and furiously defended, Tortona resisted all
Frederick's efforts for two months, and only surrendered,
when exhausted and conquered by thirst and famine,
the 6th of April 1155. The miserable citizens who
had survived were driven into exile, and the city was
given to the flames. The rumour of this event re-echoed
throughout Italy.

After the destruction of Tortona, Frederick moved
on towards Rome through Tuscany with a rapidity that
was regarded with suspicion by the Pope, who then
resided at Viterbo. The Curia began to fear that the
sovereign invoked as a protector was advancing as
an enemy. The violence from which Pascal II. had
suffered in St. Peter's less than half a century before
perhaps occurred in that hour to the mind of Hadrian.
Taking counsel with the cardinals, with Peter the
prefect of the city, and with Otho Frangipane, the

Pope sent two cardinals to meet Frederick with very clear instructions as to the terms to be come to with him. The cardinals met Frederick at St. Quirico, near Siena. Being honourably received, they expounded their mission, and showed the apostolic letters, in which, among other things, Hadrian asked to have Arnold, who had escaped from him, given back into his hands. It was a small request and easy to comply with. Frederick having had one of the barons who were protecting Arnold taken prisoner, frightened him into handing the fugitive over to the cardinals. The last hour had come for the ardent Brescian, and his premature apostolate closed in martyrdom. The prefect of Rome sentenced him to die, perhaps at Civitacastellana, but, as if to increase our pity, the precise place and day of his death are unknown. At the place of execution he did not recant, did not hesitate; mutely he breathed a prayer to God and gave himself up to the cord and the stake, calm and fearless while even the executioners wept. The Romans were prevented from preserving as relics his ashes, which were thrown into the Tiber, but his words lived fresh in their indignant memories. This martyrdom of Arnold was the seal of an alliance between the Papacy and Empire, which was destined to be short-lived and to result in nothing but bloodshed.

It had been an easy matter for Frederick to comply where only Arnold was concerned. For the rest, he said he had already sent to the Pope the archbishops Arnold of Cologne and Anselm of Ravenna to treat of the coronation and all else, nor could he give any answer before their return. And so it was; but the

Pope, on hearing of the unexpected coming of these archbishops, felt his suspicions increase, and retired to the fortified Civitacastellana, where he received them, and in his turn declared that he had sent the cardinals, and must await their return. The ambassadors had to retire on both sides and return whence they came, but meeting on the way, they decided to proceed all together to Frederick, who by this time had reached Viterbo. They did so, and in presence of the King the negotiations were concluded, and the King swore to respect the lives of the Pope and cardinals, and maintain all the stipulations. There was present at these negotiations the cardinal of St. Cecilia, Octavian, and he appears to have had a dispute with the Pope's legates. We already find him a friend of Frederick's, and an object of suspicion to the Curia, which, as we shall see, had reason not to trust him.

The conditions having been ratified by the Pope, the place and the day of solemn meeting between the two potentates were fixed. Frederick encamped in the territory of Sutri at Campo Grasso, and the Pope, reassured, and having descended from Civitacastellana to Nepi, proceeded to the King's tent, riding in the midst of his court, and of the German princes gone out to meet him. But a new event occurred to spoil the ceremony, and to reawaken suspicion in the fluttered spirits of the cardinals and Pope. Frederick did not advance to offer his services as squire to hold the Pope's bridle and stirrup. The excitement of the cardinals was extreme; the Pope, disturbed and uncertain what to do, got off his horse unwillingly, and sat on the throne prepared for him. But when

Frederick, after prostrating himself and kissing his foot, rose again to receive the customary kiss of peace, Hadrian severely and firmly refused to give it. "Thou hast deprived me," he said to the King, "of the homage which out of reverence for the apostles thy predecessors paid to mine up to our days, nor will I bestow on thee the kiss of peace till thou shalt have satisfied me." All that day and the next the dispute continued touching this special point in the ceremonial, and with such acrimony that some of the cardinals, either in anger or alarm, left the camp and retired to Civitacastellana. The steadfast firmness of the Pope carried the day. Frederick had too many reasons for not creating obstacles to his speedy coronation, and gave in. The camp was moved on a little farther to the lake of Monterosi, whither the Pope had also betaken himself by another road. Here they met again, and the King, on foot, and in the presence of the whole army, led the Pope's horse for about a stone's throw, and held his stirrup when he dismounted.

Hadrian and Frederick a few days later journeyed together to Rome, and the principal subject of their discourse was the Pope's complaints against the Romans. Near the city they were met by the ambassadors sent to Frederick by the senate and people of Rome. Full of their old dreams, they spoke in the name of Rome as lords and dispensers of that Roman Empire of which he was come to take the crown, asking him for tribute and an oath that he would guarantee the safety and liberties of the city. Frederick, having first taken counsel with the Pope and cardinals, haughtily repulsed the Roman demands. The ambassadors left the camp and returned in anger to Rome, who, like a fallen queen wounded in her pride, waited sullenly for the hour of vengeance.

The Pope, who knew the humour of the Romans, took measures accordingly. The Leonine city was in his hands, but, lest the Romans should seize it, he advised them to send on that same night a strong band of soldiers to occupy it; the Cardinal Octavian would guide and introduce them into the city. This was done. The next morning (18th of June 1155), preceded by Hadrian, who went to wait for him on the steps of the church, Frederick, at the head of his army and in great pomp, surrounded by the princes and barons, entered St. Peter's, and the Pope conducted him to worship at the shrine of the apostles. Here, according to the accustomed rites, he was crowned Roman Emperor, and under the domed roof the cheers of the Germans echoed like thunder when the imperial crown was placed on Frederick's head. The Romans, meanwhile, had crowded to the Capitol to take council how to hinder the coronation, when the news reached them that the ceremony was already accomplished. They rushed furiously to St. Peter's. From the Trastevere and the Bridge of St. Angelo they broke violently and in arms into the Leonine city, while Frederick had retired for rest to his camp outside the walls. The few soldiers who had remained behind and the Pope's and cardinal's followers were swept along and killed by the populace in its headlong career. The cardinals themselves and the Pope were in danger. The noise of the tumult reached the camp on the side where the Duke of Saxony, Henry the Lion, was resting, and he rose in a moment with his men to confront the Romans. Frederick also was instantly in arms, and with him the whole camp. A terrible contest ensued, which lasted the whole day, with great bloodshed and uncertainty. At length, towards nightfall, the dogged fury of the populace was overcome by the disciplined arms of the regular army, and the Romans were driven back across the Tiber, leaving behind them a thousand dead and some hundreds of prisoners, without reckoning the great number of wounded.

Frederick boasted of his victory, but this bloodshed neither gave him possession of the city nor assured it to Hadrian. It was out of the question to try to force an entrance into Rome, nor could he even remain where he was, as the haughty Romans refused to have any dealings with him, and he was in want of provisions for the army. He was obliged to strike his tents, and taking with him Pope and cardinals, retire into Sabina and cross the Tiber near Soracte. Thence, after a halt at the monastery of Farfa, he descended into the plains of Tivoli, to let his army rest on the banks of the Aniene, near Ponte Lucano. There, on the 29th of June, the Pope and Emperor celebrated together the feast of St. Peter and St. Paul, and it is said that on that occasion the Pope absolved the Imperialists from the blood shed in Rome, alleging that he who fights for his own prince commits no murder.

Then they moved to Albano. The Pope did not cease to urge the Emperor to march against William of Sicily and have it out with him. Nor would

Frederick perhaps have been averse to the idea, but, besides the difficulties which beset the expedition, the air of the Campagna was beginning to be felt by the troops, and the princes who had accompanied him began strongly to insist on the return home. Frederick was obliged to put off further plans, and take leave of the Pope without having made him master of Rome or protected him from William, and, in truth, leaving him in a worse condition than he was before. Hadrian was bitterly disappointed, but separated on friendly terms with the Emperor, who entered Umbria by Sabina. He met with some resistance at Spoleto, against which he already had some grounds of discontent, and taking it by assault, set fire to it. At Ancona he found the Byzantine ambassadors of the Emperor Manuel, who offered him money and assistance for the Sicilian expedition, but he could not accept them, as his return home was decided on. As far as Verona he continued his march with ease. At the locks of the Adige he found new obstacles and snares, which he overcame with great skill and courage, leaving behind him traces of stern severity to serve as a warning to those who might meditate resistance, and returned to Germany with increased reputation and the crown of Emperor. Except for this crown he had not gained much immediate advantage from his expedition; but, while the Empire had won credit and shown its strength, he had learnt to know the Italians and had made himself known to them. Once in Italy the chief stumbling-block for the Empire had been the Papacy; now the principle of municipal freedom had risen up in opposition to the principle of imperial authority and of feudal power. On one side and the other prince and people had measured their strength, now they stood in need of a tacit truce during which to prepare for the inevitable struggle.

CHAPTER IV.

(1155–1159.)

THE STRUGGLE BETWEEN HADRIAN IV. AND FREDERICK BARBAROSSA.

On his return to Germany, Frederick turned his thoughts to securing there his own greatness and that of the Empire, and to establishing power and order in the government. He made the weight of his authority sternly felt by those smaller nobles who showed themselves less submissive. He increased the power of his family by making his brother Conrad Count Palatine of the Rhine. Having divorced his first wife, Adele of Wohburg, he married Beatrice of Burgundy, and this alliance brought him the crown of Burgundy, extended his influence in Provence, and enlarged the bounds of the Empire. Thus from another side his dominions brought him nearer to Italy, whose subjection continued to occupy his thoughts and guide his policy. He settled definitely the question of the Duchy of Bavaria, and gave it to Henry the Lion, without discontenting the other pretender, the powerful Henry Jasormigott, Margrave of Austria, to please whom he raised Austria into a duchy, to which he added two provinces.   Boleslaus IV., Duke of Poland, refusing to recognise his suzerainty, he marched against him, and forced him to humble himself before him; and soon after at Würzburg the Byzantine, Bohemian, Hungarian, Danish, and English ambassadors witnessed the triumph of the young and powerful monarch. Thence proceeding with the Empress to Besançon, he set the new kingdom of Burgundy in order, and returning to Germany in January 1158, raised Ladislaw, Duke of Bohemia, to the dignity of king.   Scarcely two years had passed since his return from Italy, and the whole of Germany regarded with wonder and delight this vigorous sovereign who had done so much in so short a time.

But it was not in Germany that the destiny of the Empire could be decided, interwoven as it was with the name and fortunes of Italy, nor among so many cares did Frederick ever forget this.   Constantly since his return there reached him the complaints of the cities hostile to Milan and oppressed by her.   Pavia, Cremona, Bergamo especially invoked his aid, and he promised to hasten his return, towards which he directed all his efforts, finally determining on the second expedition for the summer of 1158.   He was incensed when he saw Milan, and other cities in her wake, taking no account of his authority, maltreating the towns faithful to him; Tortona rising from her ashes, thanks to the Milanese, and stronger than before.   Nor, while irritated with the Lombards, were his relations with the Pope all that he could wish.

Hadrian had regarded Frederick's rapid return to Germany as a desertion, and indeed he was left by it in a sad condition, disliked by the Romans and hard pressed by the King of Sicily. To these difficulties was now added the division of the cardinals into two parties, one siding with the Emperor and desirous that the Pope should enter into close alliance with him, the other suspicious of Frederick, and, remembering the long discord between Church and Empire, disposed to resume the policy of Hildebrand and make friends again with the Normans of Sicily. At the head of the first party was Octavian, cardinal of St. Cecilia, the same who had been chosen at the time of the coronation to introduce the first imperial troops into the Leonine city. The other party, to which the Pope adhered, was led by Roland, cardinal of St. Mark and chancellor of the Church, a firm, sagacious man, who, sharer in the councils and policy of Hadrian, and convinced like him of the Church's supremacy, was resolved to maintain it. A few months after Frederick's departure, towards the November of 1155, the Pope had proceeded to Benevento, aided and incited thereto by the Apulian barons, who were in rebellion against William. Thence making himself the centre of the revolt and supporting the Emperor of Constantinople, who was preparing an expedition against William, he drove this latter to such extremities that he was glad to re-enter into negotiations and offer excellent conditions of peace. The Pope inclined to accept them, but the majority of the cardinals opposed him and would not hear of peace. Soon afterwards, however, the tide turned in favour of William, who defeated the rebels and the Byzantines and threatened Benevento. There was nothing for it but to yield.

Hadrian sent Roland with other cardinals to treat, and peace was definitely concluded, though on conditions far less favourable for the Pope than the former ones.

The news of this peace, concluded without his consent, seemed to Barbarossa an infraction of the terms come to but lately before their meeting, and the growing suspicion led soon to a first rupture. While Frederick was in Burgundy, two cardinals of great authority presented themselves as legates from the Pope, the chancellor Roland, and Bernard, cardinal of St. Clement. They were received courteously, in presence of the principal barons, but the greeting with which they addressed the Emperor seemed strange to the bystanders: "The Pope and cardinals salute you, the one as father, the others as brethren;" then they handed in the papal letter. It was haughty in tone, and in it Hadrian reproached Frederick for having allowed in his states that the bishop of Lunden should be despoiled with impunity and imprisoned, and to have known of this violence and to have ignored it. That he was so much the more surprised at such a thing, as hardly a year had passed since the Roman Church had *conferred* upon him such unbounded honour and the imperial crown; nor did it regret having done so, and would have gladly been able to *benefit* him even further. He feared lest some one was perversely sowing discord between them. He concluded by recommending to him the two legates, who had full powers to treat of all matters between the Curia and Empire.

On the reading of this letter there arose an indignant uproar among the assembled barons, and a tumultuous scene followed. They were especially incensed at the allusions to the imperial dignity *conferred* by the Pontiff, and by the word *benefit* (*beneficia*). In those phrases their jealous pride dreaded some pretensions on the Pope's part to the right of conferring the crown as a gift, and almost as a feudal benefice. They angrily reminded the legates how at the time of the coronation they had heard of the painting in the Lateran representing the coronation of Lothair, with the humiliating inscription which declared him a liegeman of the Pope (*homo Papæ*), and how the latter, waiving all such pretensions, had promised that it should be cancelled. The legates did not bow before the storm—nay, one of them appears to have added fuel to the flames by exclaiming, "And from whom does the Emperor hold the Empire if not from the Pope?" The fury aroused by these words knew no bounds, and the Palatine of Bavaria, Otto of Wittelsbach, rushed with drawn sword upon the audacious legate. Frederick restrained the excitement by the authority of his presence, and with difficulty calmed the tumult, covering with his person the cardinals, who were in danger. The next morning the two legates were dismissed, with strict orders to go straight back, without stopping right or left in any bishop's palace or abbey.

Frederick felt the importance of being the first to tell the German clergy of what had happened, and hardly had the legates left when he sent his own account of it to all parts of the realm. He described the tenor of the papal letter, and the indignation which its false and detestable expressions had aroused in the princes of the Empire. He added that the legates had been sent straight back, because there had been found on them blank letters with the papal seal attached, to be filled up as they chose, and he insinuated that by their means they would have tried to despoil the altars and carry off the treasures of the German churches. The Empire was his by the election of the princes, and he held it from God alone, and it was a denial of divine institutions to affirm that he had taken the imperial crown as a benefice from the Pope. Let them all stand by him against these pretensions, for he would rather die than endure such disgrace.

It appears that the accounts given by the two cardinals on their return to the Curia and their lamentations were received in different ways by the other cardinals, according to the party to which they belonged. The Pope, at any rate, wrote to the German bishops complaining bitterly of the Emperor's conduct, and begging of them to remonstrate with him, recall him to milder councils, and obtain from him that the chancellor Rainold Dassel and Otto of Wittelsbach, as the principal offenders, should give satisfaction to the Church. But this letter was not well received, and from their answer Hadrian perceived that the bishops took the Emperor's part. Nor was it difficult to see this; the bishops, though in a respectful tone, expressed themselves clearly, and there were even signs of the answer having been written in concert with the Emperor, whose claims were once more put forward in it, and more haughtily than ever.

The bishops concluded by inviting the Pope to send fresh letters, which might conciliate the bitter feelings of the Emperor, and Hadrian saw that this was not the moment to persist. The necessity for yielding was greater because Frederick had now prepared everything for a second expedition into Italy, and was coming with a powerful army. Indeed, he had sent on ahead his chancellor, Rainold Dassel, and the count palatine Otto of Wittelsbach, to prepare the way and ensure the fidelity and assistance of the Italian cities. Two other cardinals were sent by Hadrian to meet Frederick. In June 1158 they found him at Regensburg; they presented themselves far more obsequiously than the former legates, and handed to Frederick the papal letters. In them Hadrian, after a mild complaint of the bad reception met with by his other legates, explained the unfortunate expressions of the former letter in a sense satisfactory for the Emperor. The latter accepted the explanation with apparent friendliness, and dismissed the cardinals courteously and in all honour. But Frederick's mistrust was undiminished, though he was anxious not to give Hadrian a pretext for openly joining his enemies at the moment of his descent into Italy.

In July 1158, accompanied by the King of Bohemia and the flower of the German nobles, Frederick led over the Alps the most powerful army that Italy had seen for centuries, and with it advanced into Lombardy. Brescia having offered some resistance, was soon reduced to submission by the Bohemians, who formed the vanguard; the rebuilding of Lodi, destroyed by the Milanese, was begun, and meanwhile all the cities friendly to the Emperor sent men to assist in the siege of Milan. That proud city held out for about a month, and many

deeds of valour were done on both sides. Famine,
however, soon made itself felt in the populous town,
which offered to surrender. Frederick was tolerably
moderate in the terms he demanded, but the liberties
of Milan were greatly reduced. The Milanese submitted perforce, but were secretly resolved to shake
off the yoke on the first occasion.

After receiving the homage of the Milanese, Frederick dismissed a large number of the German princes
to their homes, and proceeded to Roncaglia, where he
had convoked the Italian towns to a diet. There,
before a people who had just witnessed his immense
power, the conqueror of Milan proposed to arrange the
relations between the Empire and the cities of the
Italian realm. Never perhaps had the imperial rights
been so proudly proclaimed, and in that moment the
authority of the Empire appeared absolute in Italy,
and as if it were to last for ever. The jurists of the
various cities, under the guidance of the Bolognese
doctors and carried away by the now reawakening
memories of ancient Rome and of the Justinian Code,
proclaimed in the name of the intoxicated monarch his
absolute supremacy. Every royalty was his, his all
feudal rights, the mints, the customs, the mills, his
even the right to appoint the city consuls or to substi-
tute an officer of his own. And he who had thus been
declared lord of the whole world and whose will was
law, dictated in the diet other rules all aiming at re-
stricting the rights of the communes, adjusted differences between various cities, diminished as far as
possible the strength of the allies of Milan, from which
he also took away the lordship over Monza and the

territories of Seprio and Martesana. Frederick was near the summit of his ambition. Imperial authority had been raised in Italy to a point at which the only opponent possible was the Pope, and for him the King of Sicily could no longer offer sufficient protection. His victory was undoubted, and would be complete. Soon the glory of his empire would rival that of Charlemagne and Otto.

Frederick had not realised that he was pursuing a phantom, and that the building raised at Roncaglia rested on a foundation of sand. Soon in Lombardy the rights claimed at the diet began to seem excessive even to the friendly cities. Their friendship for the Empire, based as it was principally on their hatred of neighbouring rivals, began to waver when the Empire interfered with municipal liberties and interests. Those cities which at first combated the discontent soon began to share it. The Milanese, only half subdued by the siege, were already irritated at being deprived of territory by the decree of Roncaglia, when in January 1159 Frederick sent two legates into their city to abolish the consuls and introduce an officer of imperial appointment. The Milanese rose in tumult, and the legates had to escape by flight. The same happened at Crema when Frederick, incited to it by the entreaties and enmity of Cremona, had sent orders to dismantle the walls and fill up the trenches. Soon after the Milanese openly declared war, and took armed possession of the castle of Trezzo, making prisoners of its German garrison, and tried several times but vainly to destroy the new city of Lodi, which was being built under the auspices of the Emperor. Brescia also

C. H. D

recovered herself and joined the Milanese.   Frederick,
then at Bologna, declared the city of Milan again an
enemy of the Empire, and waited for reinforcements
from Germany.   These were brought by Henry the
Lion, who accompanied also the Empress, and by Duke
Guelph, the Emperor's uncle, who had just been invested with the lands of the Countess Matilda, to which
the Pope laid claim.   Advancing into Lombardy and
aided by Pavia and Cremona, Barbarossa began to
harass Milan and laid a cruel siege to Crema, whose
heroic defence of seven months is among the most
glorious mentioned in history.

Hadrian IV. had meanwhile begun again to quarrel
with the Emperor, and, after having yielded on one side,
offered fresh resistance on another.   The irreconcilable
principle of two supremacies rendered their two representatives irreconcilable also, and provided endless subjects of complaint.   Lately Frederick was offended
because the Pope declined to confirm the nomination
of Guido, son of Count Guido of Biandrate, whom he
wished to propose for the archbishopric of Ravenna.
Soon after a pontifical letter was brought to the Emperor by a poor-looking messenger, who disappeared
immediately after consigning it.   The letter contained
new and bitter complaints against the exactions made
by the imperial officers after the Diet of Roncaglia
on ecclesiastical possessions.   Frederick, irritated by
the tone of the letter and the unusual way it was sent,
desired his chancellor in answering it to place his
name before the Pope's, and to address him in the
second person singular.   Thus he thought to remind
the Pontiff of the old imperial supremacy, and the con-

test waxed more bitter in spite of all that Eberhard,
bishop of Bamberg, with true apostolic zeal, could do
to moderate the Pope and to soothe Frederick. " For,"
as the good bishop wrote of the latter to a cardinal,
" you know how he is. He loves those who love him,
and turns away from others, not having yet thoroughly
learnt to love also his enemies."

In order to define the differences between them, the
Pope had sent four cardinals to the Emperor, but the
terms they had to propose appeared too hard even to
the bishop of Bamberg. The Pope demanded that the
Emperor should not send officers to Rome without his
knowledge, because there all magistracy and royalties
belonged to St. Peter. The possessions of the Pope
must not be subject to forage for the imperial troops
except at the time of the coronation. The Italian
bishops only owe the Emperor the oath of allegiance,
not that of vassalage, and the imperial ambassadors
are not to be entertained in the bishops' palaces.
Restitution must be made to the Pope of the possessions of the Roman Church at Tivoli, Ferrara, Massa,
Figheruolo, all the lands of the Countess Matilda, the
territory from Acquapendente to Rome, the duchy of
Spoleto, and the islands of Sardinia and Corsica.
After long and various discussions and many complaints
that Hadrian had broken the conditions by making
friends with the King of Sicily, Frederick, in repelling
these enormous pretensions, ended by saying, not without irony, that he should not require the oath of vassalage from the Italian bishops if they would give up the
temporalities which were a royalty ; that the imperial
ambassadors would have no right to be entertained in

the bishops' palaces were it not that these, being built
on allodial land, were in reality royal palaces.   Then
the Pope's affirmation that imperial officers could not
be sent to Rome, and that the magistracy and the
royalties there were papal, would involve such loss of
all power in Rome, that the Roman Emperor would be
a mere phantom sovereign, bearing an empty name.

While these matters were being discussed, there
came to Frederick's court some ambassadors from the
city of Rome to offer him peace and recognition of his
imperial rights in return for his recognition and protection of the senate.   Frederick received gladly these
ambassadors, who arrived so opportunely, and dismissed
them honourably, and not without hopes.   At the
same time he proposed to the legates that for the
settlement of their dispute the Pope should appoint
six cardinals, he would name six bishops, and their
decision should be regarded as final.   Moreover, he
announced that he would send some ambassadors commissioned to treat with the Pope and the Romans.
In this account taken of the Romans there was an
implied threat for Hadrian, but this latter held out
firmly, and refused all arbitration, alleging that he, as
supreme Pontiff, could not submit to the judgment of
others.   The ambassadors could arrange nothing with
him or with the Romans, who probably suspected that
the Emperor wanted, under the name of prefect, to
introduce a magistrate of his own into the city, and
destroy the authority, if not the name, of the senate.
Frederick's hostility to municipal freedom injured him
on every side, and Hadrian, perceiving that this freedom contained a principle of great strength, determined

to make use of it, and addressed himself to the Lombard communes, encouraging them in their resistance. During the siege of Crema a first attempt at a league was made between the people of Milan, Brescia, and Piacenza, who agreed in Anagni with Hadrian to come to no terms without his consent or that of his successors. The besieged citizens of Crema sent their oath to the same effect. The Pope, for his part, made the same promises to the leagued city, and even announced to them that within forty days he would have excommunicated their enemy. But while Hadrian was preparing to hurl his maledictions against Frederick's arms, a sudden illness carried him off, the 1st of September 1159. A dark future lay before the Church.

CHAPTER V.

(1159–1168.)

ALEXANDER III. AND THE LOMBARDS AGAINST THE SCHISM AND THE EMPIRE.

WHEN the body of Hadrian IV. had been brought to Rome and buried in St. Peter's, the cardinals met in that church to elect the new Pope. The two parties into which they were divided confronted each other without a restraining hand over them, and on this election depended the complete victory of one or other side and the future direction of the Church's policy. Agreement was hardly possible. The majority inclined to the election of the Cardinal Roland, who favoured the Sicilian alliance, and would doubtless carry on the policy of Hadrian, but the minority offered a determined resistance, and proposed instead the Cardinal Octavian. At last, after three days' struggle, on the 7th of September 1159, Roland was elected, but the other side did not accept its defeat, and declared for their part Octavian to be Pope. The confusion was at its height, and Octavian throwing himself on the papal mantle with which the other cardinals were investing Roland, and tearing it from them, tried to carry it off, but a senator

who was present took it away from him. However, his
partisans produced another mantle, which had been prepared in secret, and two of his chaplains arrayed him in
it. Then the doors of the church being thrown open, a
band of Octavian's armed followers entered, and he was
proclaimed Pope under the name of Victor IV. The
cardinals who had elected Roland were alarmed, and
dreading violence, they retired into the fortress an-
nexed to the church, and remained shut in there for
several days, being prevented from moving by the arms
of the opposite faction. At last, for fear they should be
liberated by their friends, they were conducted thence
under a false pretence to a safer place in the Trastevere, but it availed nothing. Three days later, Roland
succeeded in escaping with his followers, was received
triumphantly and with acclamations by his party, but
was not strong enough to remain in Rome. He left
the city, followed by a large number of clergy and
people, and stopped at Ninfa, where he was consecrated
Pope as Alexander III.; then, after a short stay at
Terracina, he went to Anagni. Neither could Octavian
hold out long in Rome. His consecration took place
in the monastery of Farfa, whence he went to Segni.
Thus, in order to keep near Rome, the two rivals
quartered themselves but a few miles distant from
each other in the Campagna. Then they began to
hurl excommunications at each other, and another
schism rent the Church. To succeed in the struggle,
each rival had to persuade Christendom of the validity
of his election. Both immediately sent legates and
letters to sovereigns and bishops, each telling the story
in his own way and declaring himself the true Pope

and his adversary a schismatic. In the uncertainty, Frederick's decision might have great weight from his power in Italy and Germany, his influence throughout Europe, and his position as temporal head of Christendom. So both turned to him, but with very different hopes and feelings. Alexander III. mistrusted him, feeling that he was not acceptable, while Octavian, having always shown himself an imperialist and an enemy of Sicily, hoped for his support. And even if Frederick was really sorry for the schism, he could hardly help leaning towards Octavian. Either on a hint from the Emperor, or more probably of their own accord, the two imperial ambassadors who happened to be in Rome at the time of the election took part with Octavian, while in the letters which this latter and his partisans sent to the bishops and princes of the Empire we continually find the accusation against Alexander and his cardinals of being allied with the King of Sicily and conspiring against the Empire. The tone of Alexander III.'s letters is more independent and elevated, but they betray a conviction that the imperial sympathies are with his rival; and, indeed, the cardinals in writing to tell Frederick of the event say so openly: "May it be known to your sublime grace that Otto, Count Palatine, taking advantage of Octavian's intrusion, gave great molestation to our aforesaid lord and ourselves, and tried to divide the Church of God and to disturb it in many ways. For he violently entered the Campagna and patrimony of St. Peter with the intruder and apostate Octavian, trying in every way to make the land subject to him. . . . Consider that you, in the office of your imperial dignity, should protect the Church and defend her from her opponents, and above all from heretics and schismatics. Our wish is to honour you as the special defender and patron of the Roman Church, and, as far as in us lies, we desire with God the increase of your glory. Therefore, we supplicate you to love and honour the Holy Roman Church your mother, to watch over her peace and tranquillity, as it becomes the imperial excellence, and not to favour in any way the great iniquity of this invading schismatic." Even in these anxious moments the traditions left by Hadrian IV., were still in force and the prayers of the cardinals to Frederick sounded almost like admonitions.

But Frederick was not disposed to listen. Placed between the two pretenders, he seized the opportunity which Lothair in the former schism had neglected, and looking backwards at the examples left him by his earliest predecessors, he aspired to be arbitrator in this great struggle. By this he hoped to place again on their former footing ecclesiastical rights, which had gradually been changing and seeking emancipation from the authority of the Empire. He therefore decided to convoke a council and intimate to the two rivals to appear before it and make good their claims. Two bishops were commissioned to carry the letters of invitation. In them Frederick said that the care and protection of the Church had been committed to him by God, and that he was greatly grieved by the schism. In order to settle it, he summoned a council to meet at Pavia, and convoked to it all the bishops and clergy not only of the imperial states, but also of other realms. The council would judge the question

freely, and he, in the name of God and the Catholic
Church, commanded them to present themselves before
it to hear the decision. The two messengers carried
these letters, while other letters from Frederick invited
the bishops and the higher clergy of Europe to the
council. The position of Alexander III. was extremely delicate, for in refusing he might appear to
have doubts as to his cause, and would give an easy
pretext for Frederick's open enmity and for an alliance
between him and Octavian. Yet a refusal was un-
avoidable. Both he and his cardinals were convinced
of Frederick's hostility, and they also felt that to
accept would be to destroy with their own hands the
principle of a Church free from and superior to all
earthly authority. After a long consultation with the
cardinals, Alexander replied to Frederick's envoys that
he recognised in the Emperor the special defender
of the Church, and would honour him above all other
princes, but that to honour him he could not offend
God. That he wondered at Frederick's want of reverence to the Church, which he, Alexander, represented.
His proposal was unprecedented. He was overstepping
the limits of the imperial dignity in convoking a
council without the Pope's knowledge, and summoning
him as if he had any power whatever over the Pontiff.
God had willed that he should be subject to no one,
and he could not present himself before the imperial
court without incurring, through ignorance or cowardice,
the risk of enslaving that Church for whose liberty
his predecessors had died, and for whom he too
was ready if necessary to lay down his life. This
was Alexander's answer; Octavian, on the other

hand, accepted the invitation and betook himself to Pavia.

Finally, after a siege of many months, Crema had to cease from her heroic defence and surrendered. Frederick, in what he called his extreme clemency, spared the citizen's lives ; those unhappy heroes were driven forth and their city destroyed. He then opened the council at Pavia with a speech to the bishops, in which, notwithstanding some intentional vagueness, his ideas of the relations between the Empire and the Church came out clearly enough. " In my office and dignity of Emperor," he said, " I can convoke councils, especially in moments of grave peril for the Church, as did Constantine, Theodosius, Justinian, and in later times the emperors Charlemagne and Otto. But I leave it to your prudence and power to decide regarding this most weighty matter ; for God made you priests and gave you power to judge us also. And since in the things which belong to God it is not for us to judge you, we exhort you to act in this cause as in one which appertains to God alone, and we await your judgment."

Having said these words, he retired and left them to their deliberations. Besides a large number of abbots and minor ecclesiastics, there were at this council about fifty, between bishops and archbishops, chiefly from Germany and North Italy, for from other countries hardly any had accepted the invitation. Octavian had an easy victory. The prelates who had come were predisposed in his favour, and he being present, could himself defend his cause and call witnesses. Alexander, on the contrary, did not recognise the council, and had no one to defend him, while besides the canonical objections which were made to him, there were other not unfounded accusations of his conspiring against the Empire and in favour of the Sicilian kingdom and of the Lombards.   Octavian was declared Pope on the 11th of February 1160, being honoured as such by council and Emperor; the following day he solemnly excommunicated Roland and his followers, and admonished William of Sicily and the Milanese as invaders of the rights of Church and Empire.

This blow did not shake Alexander.   First of all, as a declaration of open war, he excommunicated Frederick and renewed the anathemas against Octavian and his accomplices.   In this way he proudly proclaimed his authority, and in freeing the subjects of the Empire from all duty of obedience and fealty, he encouraged the revolt of the Lombards and created divisions in Germany.   A clever and energetic diplomatist, he sent continually to the bishops in all parts of Europe letters combining dignity with insinuating gentleness, defending his rights and urging them to plead for the same before people and kings.   He was specially anxious to obtain the recognition of the courts of France and England, and was supported in this by the French, Norman, and English bishops.   And in truth Frederick, in spite of many efforts, could not get the sovereigns of these two countries to abandon a reserve which was if anything favourable to Alexander, and which later changed into an open recognition of his claim.

The cruel fate of Crema had not diminished the Lombards' aversion to imperial rule nor their resistance, which their alliance with the Pope served to forward in every way. Milan, Brescia, Piacenza were in arms, and Barbarossa determined to cut the knot by destroying Milan. It was a long and arduous undertaking ; nor would he have succeeded but for the assistance of those Lombard cities whose municipal jealousy aroused a blind fury against their powerful sister. For a whole year there was constant warfare round Milan, with alternating results and a cruel destruction of the vast surrounding plain. Then towards the spring of 1161, after the arrival of reinforcements from Germany and Hungary, the town was shut in more closely and an atrocious siege lasted for another year. At length the flower of the resisting forces being killed, disease and hunger having done their worst, the last munitions being consumed, Milan surrendered at discretion. The fall and misery of the great city touched even her enemies, and they invoked for her Frederick's clemency ; but the stern statesman met their supplications with a countenance of stone. He felt the necessity of a terrible example which might once for all stifle every hope of resistance. Milan was utterly destroyed by pillage and fire, and seemed to have disappeared for ever from the face of the earth.

To those Milanese who survived the siege were assigned four localities where they might settle, not very far from the ruined city. It would have been difficult to provide for them otherwise, yet a contemporary chronicler reproached Frederick afterwards with his mistake in leaving the Milanese so near their old home as to be tempted to rebuild it. But how could he have feared it then ? The power of Barbarossa was

at that time unbounded in Lombardy. Piacenza and
Brescia, giving up all idea of resistance, accepted his
hard conditions, dismantled their walls, received the imperial officers, gave money and hostages, and recognised
the Emperor's Pope, while the bishop of Piacenza, who
opposed him, went to rejoin Alexander III. in exile.
Many other cities submitted to the potent monarch, and
the imperial rights proclaimed some years before at
Roncaglia were at last in full force. The Lombard
cities, in losing their dearly-prized liberty, were reap-
ing the fruit of their discords. It was a bitter fruit,
but destined to act upon them as a healing medicine.

After the subjection of Lombardy and the firmer foot-
hold gained in Northern Italy, it seemed easier for
Frederick to realise his plan of extending his rule, or
at least his direct influence, over the whole of the peninsula; but Alexander III.'s strong yet flexible nature
was always there to oppose his designs. While he was
fighting in Lombardy, Alexander, except for a short
stay in Rome, rendered soon untenable by his adversaries, had remained in the Campagna, harassed by
the imperial troops, which had taken possession of
almost the whole patrimony of St. Peter. Gradually all
Europe and the East had recognised him, leaving Frederick alone in his support of Octavian, but the difficulty
of holding out in the Campagna, notwithstanding support from Sicily, increased, so that he resolved to leave
Italy. Accompanied by his court, he betook himself to
France, the faithful refuge of exiled Popes, thinking
truly that he could thence exercise a more direct influence on the French and English kings, and counter-
act the activity of the Emperor against him. Having

embarked at Capo Circello on board the Sicilian galleys, he stopped at Genoa, and entering France by
Provence, was received everywhere with great honours.
Writing from Genoa to Eberhard, bishop of Salzburg,
who was his stoutest champion in Germany, he exhorted him to admonish the Emperor to abandon the
schism and return to the Church, when all past wrongs
would be forgotten. But while he offered peace he did
not suspend warfare, and soon after, in the spring of
1162, at Montpellier he solemnly repeated the sentence
of excommunication, against Octavian and Frederick;
also, while trying everywhere in Germany and Italy
to draw all men over to his cause, he incited the clergy
in a thousand ways to resist Octavian, which meant
resisting Frederick. This latter had convoked two
more synods at Lodi and Cremona, and in both the
decisions of the synod of Pavia were confirmed; but he
could not avoid seeing that among the German and
Italian bishops Alexander's adherents continued to increase, either openly or in secret, and that even among
those most obsequious to himself many accepted Octavian with reserve. He therefore resolved, at whatever
cost, to overthrow his dangerous adversary, and as a
first step tried to deprive him of his present asylum.

After so prolonged an absence, Frederick felt that
his return to Germany was imperative, and indeed
Lombardy was so wasted that an army could no longer
subsist there. He deputed some officers to hold the
province and keep it down, and then crossed the Alps,
but not before he had addressed Louis VII. of France,
profiting by the threatening attitude of England, to try
to gain him over to himself and separate him entirely

from the Pope.   Louis hesitated; by nature irresolute, and advised by some round him who were in favour of an alliance with the Emperor, he treated with Frederick, and even entered into relations with Octavian, but without breaking with Alexander, who, however, saw what was going on and felt anxious.   It was settled that on the 29th of August 1162 Frederick and Louis should have an interview on the banks of the Saöne near St. Jean de Losne, where the French kingdom adjoined Burgundy, which was subject to Frederick.   Henry of Troyes, brother-in-law of the king, who wished for the alliance in order to estrange Louis from Henry II. of England, agreed to certain conditions for the interview. The two sovereigns were to bring with them the two pretenders to the papacy, and to recognise as the true Pope the one judged to be such by the highest magnates of the two realms, both ecclesiastical and lay.   If one of the pretenders should decline to appear, the claims of the other should be acknowledged without further delay.   Later the King of France asserted that Henry of Troyes went beyond his instructions, and had no authority to agree to such conditions.   Meanwhile Alexander, perceiving the serious danger of such an interview, did all in his power to hinder it, and besieged with letters and messengers all those who might directly or indirectly influence the king.   He partly succeeded, for he himself had an interview with Louis only a few days before he was to meet the Emperor. He could not dissuade the king from the meeting, but he was able to convince him that he, the Vicar of Christ, could not bow before any human tribunal, and instead of accompanying him himself, he sent some cardinals with him to support his cause, and left the king well secured against the imperial flatteries.

The King of France advanced hesitatingly towards the banks of the Saône, anxious not to keep the incautious promises of Henry of Troyes, but uncertain how to act. He also had suspicions of Frederick, who, besides his Pope, the King of Denmark, and a great many other bishops and princes, brought with him a considerable army. Frederick also had his suspicions, and foresaw Alexander's influence on the mind of Louis. However, early on the day fixed, he presented himself with Victor IV. on the bridge where the meeting was to take place, but not finding the king there, he retired. Later Louis arrived, and without waiting to see whether the Emperor would return, he also promptly departed.

Thus the interview did not take place, perhaps because neither of the princes wished for it. But the next day, at Dijon, Henry of Troyes, by threatening to transfer his allegiance to the Emperor, induced Louis to promise again that he would return in three weeks for a colloquy, and would, as well as the Emperor, accept the decision of a congress. This promise disturbed Alexander. It was out of the question he should yield and present himself at that congress; and he now saw Louis falling into the hands of the Emperor. But he did not lose heart. He redoubled his instances, so that if the King of France could not avoid Frederick, he might at least not be shaken by him; and in order to detach Louis from every idea of an imperial alliance, he made efforts to draw over to him the King of England, who, at least for the moment, and for the sake of hindering an alliance dangerous to himself also, willingly seconded these efforts. This clever move disconcerted Frederick. His meeting with the king did not take place; for in his discouragement he began to think of retiring, not being in a position to enter suddenly on a campaign against the two monarchs who were entering into an alliance before his eyes. He did not go to meet the king, and sent in his stead his chancellor, Dassel, who refused to recognise the conditions agreed to; so that Louis, declaring himself free from every obligation towards the Emperor, turned his back on the chancellor and returned to Dijon, glad to have got off so easily.

Before leaving Burgundy for Germany, Frederick held a diet at Dôle, in which Victor IV. defended afresh the validity of his election, and repeated his excommunication of Alexander. But the skilful policy of this latter assured him a triumph at this time. After a meeting with Henry II. of England at Chateauroux, he saw him again, a few days later, at Couci-sur-Loire, together with the King of France. There the two monarchs, with great ostentation of reverential homage, solemnly proclaimed, before the Empire and the world, that the Pontiff who had united them was the true Pope; and Alexander's position as head of Christendom was assured. The rivalry of Octavian, who was no longer formidable, thus almost disappeared, and the struggle, losing its personal character, became again one of vast interests and principles between the Papacy and the Empire. This was now to be the great object of all Alexander's and Frederick's most tenacious efforts.

Though transferred for a moment to France, the

real seat of this struggle was always Italy, and on it
was fixed the gaze of the two sagacious adversaries,
though neither of them could return there just then.
Frederick was obliged to stay some time longer in
Germany, where much internal discord required his
restraining hand. Lombardy meanwhile was being
cruelly oppressed. The imperial officers, without
mercy or restraint, and with a rapacity that knew
no bounds, were wringing the last drop from those
populations, already chafing at the loss of their liberties. The victims, suffering from every form of griev-
ance and hardship, vainly pleaded for justice; the only
answer to their supplications were heavier burdens
and increased extortions. The recent recollection
of defeat and the terrible example of Milan warned
them to be patient, so that the unhappy provinces
were reduced to wishing for Frederick's return, thinking that the sight of their miseries would move him
to relieve them. False hope! Barbarossa returned
with a small army, but he paid little heed to the
lamentations which resounded on all sides, and the
oppression grew daily more grievous. The measure of
sorrow and suffering was heaped up. While Frederick
was engaged in appointing one of his creatures as
king in Sardinia, without estranging Genoa and Pisa,
who were disputing with each other the possession of
the island, some signs of resistance began to appear.
Encouraged by Venice and leagued together, Verona,
Padua, and Vicenza revolted, and swore to defend each
other mutually, and not to yield to the Empire any
right not included in ancient custom. This was the
nucleus of a wider league; and Barbarossa, who felt

this, and had no sufficient army with him to quell
those cities, sought to pacify them; but the attempt
failed. Calling in the assistance of Pavia, Mantua,
and Ferrara, which he loaded with privileges, he tried
to advance against the allies, which had been joined
by Treviso and a tract of the neighbouring country;
but they presented themselves in such strong force
that he was obliged to retire without risking a battle.

In the meantime the ecclesiastical questions had
become further complicated. The antipope, Octavian,
had died at Lucca, and the chancellor, Rainald Dassel,
archbishop of Cologne, a fierce imperialist, and afraid,
perhaps, that the Emperor himself might come to
terms with Alexander III., obtained the election of
one of the two remaining schismatic cardinals, Guido
of Crema, who took the name of Paschal III. Frederick accepted him as true Pope, and tried hard, after
his return to Germany, to get him recognised by the
Italian and German bishops. In both countries, however, he found the whole episcopate not only hesitating,
but opposed to an election with so little pretension to
legality. Conrad of Wittelsbach, archbishop-elect of
Mentz, rather than yield, went into exile in France
near Alexander; the archbishops of Trier and Magdeburg, the bishops of Salzburg and Brixen, held out;
many others submitted in appearance only to the
imperial will. This ecclesiastical opposition, which
increased the turmoil of fresh discords in Germany
then harassing the Empire, was well known to the
Lombards and encouraged them.

Nor was it from this side only that encouragement
came. Alexander III. had not remained inactive all

this time, and after visiting at Paris the King of France, who received him with great honour, he had called a council at Tours, to which bishops from all parts had presented themselves, and even many of the Germans had written to Alexander giving in their secret adherence. Having thus strengthened his own position and cut off Octavian from all support except that of the Emperor, he began to feel his way towards a reconciliation with the latter; but Frederick brought up again the question of the legality of the election, insisting on its being decided by arbitration, so that the negotiations soon came to an end. Then Alexander carried on the struggle, and did all he could to keep alive the wrath of Lombardy. His letters written from France, and those of the prelates who followed his fortunes, show what hopes he placed in the league of the Lombards and in their undaunted spirit of revolt and of resistance to servitude. By open and by secret means he animated them, and at the same time did not lose sight of the other courts, trying to be on friendly terms with them and to destroy their confidence in Frederick. With Louis of France, with the court of Sicily, he was closely allied, while he had constant communications with the Emperor of Constantinople and with Venice, both declared enemies of Barbarossa. He made continual efforts to draw all these powers into closer harmony in favour of the Church, while Frederick, feeling his isolation and the network of enmity which surrounded him, was watching for the point where he could best break through and destroy it.

Henry II. of England, in spite of the homage paid to the Pope at Couci-sur-Loire, had not remained a

devout and steadfast adherent like Louis VII. Besides
its being very difficult for the Pope to be equally acceptable to two potentates who had so many motives
of mutual suspicion, a serious cause of discontent had
arisen between Alexander and Henry. It grew out of
that jealous care characteristic of English history in the
Middle Ages, with which the royal prerogatives were
guarded against ecclesiastical interference, and which
was at that moment maintained with extreme rigour.
We must touch upon it here only on account of its influence on the relations between Church and Empire. The
contest which William Rufus had sustained with the
gentle but inflexible piety of Anselm was now repeated
with more bitterness between men of very different tempers. Thomas Becket, when he succeeded the learned
and prudent Theobald in the see of Canterbury, had
altered his habits, not his character, which was noble
but excessive even in good, and pugnacious in spite
of frequent gleams of humility and charity. To the
struggle between the archbishop of Canterbury and
the King of England Alexander could not remain
indifferent, and as in the interests of the Church of
Canterbury were involved the interests and principles
of the universal Church, the Pope supported the archbishop. But it was a delicate matter. The king had
warm and not disinterested friends in the Curia and
among the Pope's most influential counsellors, while a
not inconsiderable part of the English clergy were
adverse to Becket, whose defence was rendered more
difficult by his often intemperate zeal. Add to this
—and hence the connection between this important
ecclesiastical episode and our history—that the schism,

though less threatening, was not yet entirely quenched, and might still, not probably but possibly, be rekindled if Henry joined the Emperor and succeeded in carrying with him part of his clergy.

Nor did Frederick omit to seek an alliance with the King of England, and this latter, taking advantage of the opportunity, responded to his advances, and continued in this way to threaten Alexander until the final tragic scene of this controversy with Becket. Still this alliance, which deprived Alexander of a strong support and rendered the greatest circumspection necessary in his dealings with the English king, did not essentially change Frederick's position in his struggle with the Pope. This latter was now well rooted in his place, and though he might be shaken, he could not be overturned, and intended now to re-enter Italy and find himself on the principal battlefield. As soon as his vicar, the cardinal of Saints John and Paul, had gained for him so much loyalty among the Romans as secured his being able to stay in Rome, Alexander left the hospitable coast of France in September 1165, and in November touched at Messina. The King of Sicily sent him rich gifts from Palermo, and gave orders that five galleys and some important personages of the realm should accompany him to Rome. He was received there with solemn pomp, and amid the acclamations of the people went in procession to take up his abode in the Lateran. It was the sixth year of his pontificate.

Frederick had returned some time before to Germany, and while trying to strengthen order and government, he was intent on preparing such an army as might once for all, if led into Italy, put a stop to the innumerable hindrances which met him from one end to the other of the peninsula. With his mind full of the majesty of the Holy Roman Empire, he had wished to reawaken reverence for it in other minds by procuring special honours for its great founder, whom he admired and longed to imitate. Paschal III. canonised Charlemagne on the Christmas-day of 1165 at Aix-la-Chapelle; but that hero did not rise from his uncovered tomb, nor did his times return. The ages had brought great changes. Papacy, Empire, and people, and the entire atmosphere of thoughts and hopes that surrounded them, were no longer the same; different also was the arduous and less fruitful labour which destiny had reserved for Barbarossa's tenacious spirit.

Encouraged by his absence, the Lombards took up an attitude of more open defiance. The troops were often insufficient to suppress the frequent tumults in the subject cities, and at Bologna the imperial lieutenant was even killed by the populace. In Sicily the death of William I., to whom, under his mother's regency, succeeded William II., later called the Good, had not altered the friendly understanding with the Pope. On the contrary, this was strengthened, and to a certain extent it was cemented, by the Emperor Manuel of Constantinople, who, hostile to Barbarossa, and anxious to take his place in Italy, paid court to both the young prince and the Pope, flattering this latter with the mirage of reunion with the Greek Church, and asking in exchange the Roman crown of Empire. Alexander, prudent, and incredulous of the result, began nevertheless negotiations with a view to isolating Frederick and causing him anxiety. Venice, Sicily, and Constantinople were united in a common object, and were masters of the Adriatic, while in the Mediterranean, Pisa, and still more Genoa, though friendly to the Emperor, could not always be depended on. Therefore, with the sea shut in great part against him, and with opposition in the interior, it had become necessary for him to reconquer Italy or to abandon her altogether. He sent on ahead with the vanguard the archbishop of Cologne, Rainald Dassel, and followed himself, determined to strike a decisive blow. Rainald moved towards Rome, and encamping round it, drew over a large part of the Campagna into obedience to Paschal III., then residing at Viterbo, which had become a centre of operations for the imperialists. Barbarossa, on his descent into Lombardy, devastated the districts of Brescia and Bergamo, then advancing, avenged at Bologna the death of his lieutenant, ravaged Romagna, and stationed himself before Ancona, which was a key to the Adriatic, and the safest harbour for the Greek fleets. By seizing on this town he hoped to give a death-blow to Byzantine interests, and to place himself in a commanding position between Venice and Sicily. The siege of Ancona began.

He met with stout resistance; while in Lombardy the league of Verona had set an example, which early in 1167 Bergamo, Brescia, Cremona, and Mantua followed. Soon afterwards the dispersed citizens of Milan swore to the conditions of the famous league, which was to rescue Lombardy, and, when it was formed, its members met again at the abbey of Pontida for the discussion of their projects. Putting aside their fraternal enmity to the queen of Lombard cities, they decided that Milan must be rebuilt, and raised as a war-standard against the oppressor. On April 27, 1167, the troops of the confederates appeared before the fallen city, to assist in her reconstruction, and to defend her in case of attack on the part more especially of Pavia, the faithful ally of the Empire. Milan rose from her ruins. The league began to spread, other towns joined it, and on every side fortifications were raised, walls rebuilt, preparations were made for war, and men's hearts beat high.

The Pope gave his warmest blessing to this zeal and harmony, in which he saw his surest support in present difficulties. He scattered all the gold he had among the leading men in Rome, and was regarded with a friendly eye by the Romans in general, thanks to their hatred of the neighbouring cities, who favoured the Empire, and especially of Tusculum. The republican rule in Rome had encouraged the formation of a city militia so numerous as to give some anxiety to the archbishop of Cologne, who found himself at Tusculum with insufficient forces. The Emperor sent him reinforcements led by another archbishop, Christian of Buch, a clever and very warlike man, whom he had intruded into Mentz in place of Conrad of Wittelsbach. The Romans, deaf to the Pope's dissuasions, advanced boldly and in great numbers against the two archbishops to Monte Porzio on the Tusculan hills, but being surrounded, suffered a tremendous defeat, and escaping with difficulty, were pursued as far as Rome, leaving the battlefield and the line of flight strewn with corpses. The discouragement and distress were great, and funeral lamentations filled the streets. The Pope, on seeing the danger, collected what soldiers he could, had the weaker parts of the wall strengthened and prepared for resistance, as the imperial troops were already encamped before the city. Frederick, entreated by the archbishop of Mentz, made peace with Ancona, and advancing rapidly, appeared with his army on the heights of Monte Mario. The following day, coming down the hill, he attempted to storm the walls, but was repulsed by the Pope's soldiers. After another furious assault behind the castellated church of St. Peter, the imperialists, enraged by resistance, made good their entrance. The neighbouring church of St. Maria in Torri was set fire to, and the flames attacked the vestibule of the very basilica. The Emperor's nephew, Frederick of Rotenburg, son of King Conrad III., a handsome and courageous knight, amidst blinding flames broke open the temple doors with his battle-axe, and the armed tide, among the rest the two archbishops, burst in, spreading blood and slaughter up to the polluted tomb of the apostles. Fearing the complete destruction of the church, the Papal troops surrendered. Then the antipope was hastily enthroned there, and the Emperor had the Empress crowned with great pomp.

The left bank of the Tiber was not yet in Barbarossa's hands. The Pope, who some time before had retired near the Coliseum, where the Frangipane were fortified, was in constant communication with the cardinals and bishops as to what could be done in such a strait. The King of Sicily had lately sent by the Tiber two galleys

and a large sum of money, to be used, the former for
flight, the second for defence, according as they were
needed. Alexander distributed the money among the
Roman nobles who were on his side, and among the
guards at the gates, and sent away the galleys with two
cardinals, but would not himself abandon Rome. In
that dark hour he still felt himself strong, and perhaps
did not despair of coming to at least a temporary understanding with Frederick while the Romans continued
to support him. Certainly he allowed Conrad of Wittelsbach, the fugitive archbishop of Mentz, to pay the
Emperor a visit. This latter, seizing the opportunity,
commissioned Conrad to propose to the bishops and
cardinals that Alexander and Paschal should both of
them give up the Papacy, and that a third person should
be chosen freely in their stead. He also informed the
Romans of his proposal, promising if it was carried into
effect to return all the prisoners and the booty that
remained after the defeat of Monte Porzio. The bishops
and cardinals unanimously and unhesitatingly rejected
this proposal, but the people urged that Alexander
should give way, in order to save his flock in this
emergency, and should give up the Papacy. Alexander,
after secretly taking counsel with a few cardinals, suddenly disappeared. Three days later he was seen with
some attendant taking refreshment at the foot of Monte
Circello, then by Terracina and Gaeta he retired to
Benevento, where the cardinals who had remained
behind joined him, clinging to their head, says Alexander's biographer, as limbs of a single body.

When Alexander had left the town, the Romans

made terms with Frederick, taking an oath of obedience, and subordinating to his authority the appointment and power of the senate. The appearance on the Tiber of eight Pisan galleys contributed probably to overcome their opposition, as also the announced approach of a large fleet of ships ready at a signal from the Emperor to attack Rome and Sicily. The power of Frederick had now reached its summit. Master of Rome, with the Pope a fugitive, strong in his own arms and in the Pisan ships, he was preparing to attack the King of Sicily, utterly crush his forces, then return to quell the rebellious Lombards, and having at length made himself master of Italy, he would show himself to the world as the real head of the revived Empire of Charlemagne. Destiny willed otherwise. It was now August; the sun was burning the arid Campagna and oppressing the weary German troops. A slight rain came to refresh them, but the following day sudden destruction fell upon the camp. Deadly fever attacked the army with terrible violence and reduced it daily. The men fell in heaps, and when struck down in the morning were dead by night. The disease took stronger hold owing to the superstitious fears of the army and the idea of divine vengeance, for the soldiers remembered in terror the profanation of St. Peter's, and they felt the keen edge of the destroying angel's sword. Decimated, dismayed, demoralised, the imperial army was hopelessly defeated, and Frederick was compelled to strike his tents and fly before the invisible destroyer. Pursued by this foe, he led what remained of his unfortunate forces towards the Tuscan highlands, losing great

numbers by the way. The flower of his troops lay
unburied in the furrows, and with difficulty could he
manage to carry back to their native land the bodies
of his noblest and trustiest knights. Never perhaps
before had Frederick given proofs of such unshaken
strength of mind. The most tenacious supporters of
his plans, the most valiant sharers of his perils, had
fallen one by one before that inglorious foe. The high
chancellor-archbishop of Cologne, Rainald Dassel, was
a corpse, and stiffened in death lay the arm of young
Frederick of Suabia, who but a few days before had
struck so vigorously at the portals of St. Peter's. The
bishops of Liège, Spires, Ratisbon, Verden all dead,
dead also Duke Guelph of Bavaria, and hundreds of
other nobles and churchmen. On this desolate march
Frederick dragged along the survivors as best he could
with him into Tuscany, and delayed there but a few
days while the disease still lingered among them. Not
being able to follow the usual roads, which were barred
by the Lombards in arms, he took to the hills, and by
rough paths reached Pavia. Having gathered together
the scattered remnants, and assisted by some city still
faithful, by the Count of Biandrate and the Marquis of
Montferrat, he attempted in some small engagements
to ravage the Milanese territory during the winter; but
the superior forces of Lombardy enclosed him as in an
iron ring, so that he had to make use of craft to get
out of Italy in safety. Under the protection of Hum-
bert, Count of Maurienne, he arrived with a few men
at Susa, whence, owing to the threats of the citizens
risen in revolt, he had great difficulty in escaping by

night across the Alps. He returned to Germany alone and almost a fugitive, his bravest knights dead, his army destroyed, and leaving behind him a whole nation of proud and watchful enemies. He returned alone, but his spirit was undaunted and dreamt of future victory and of final revenge.

CHAPTER VI.

(1168–1181.)

THE BATTLE OF LEGNANO AND THE PEACE OF VENICE—DEATH OF ALEXANDER III.

THE absence of Barbarossa did not lull to sleep the courageous activity of the leagued Lombards, who made their preparations in expectation of his return. The league spread rapidly, and in a short time the greater part of the cities and territories of Venetia, Lombardy, and Piedmont were in a confederation against the Emperor, against those cities like Pavia which still sided with him, and against the feudal lords. Having tried their strength in some engagements, such as the taking of the castle of Biandrate, the cities of the league determined, as a greater safeguard against any future invading army, to build a strong city on the spot where the waters of the Tanaro and Bormida unite, in such a position as to guard almost every entrance into Lombardy. This city rose with astonishing rapidity, and many flocked to it, so that in a short time it numbered 15,000 inhabitants. The aim of its foundation was sufficiently marked by the name of Alessandria, which it received in honour of

Alexander III. This Pope never ceased to encourage the confederates, assisted by the Lombard clergy, who were headed by Galdinus, the archbishop of Milan, a sworn enemy of the Emperor and the antipope. Thus while the League grew stronger, everything else in Italy was also going against the Empire. Pisa and Genoa, always suspicious of each other, and often in open conflict, attended far more to their own than to the imperial interests. Nay, Genoa, without actually joining the League, regarded it with favour, and even helped it with money, while both the republics, each on its own account, had entered into friendly negotiations with the King of Sicily, although as yet without result. William II., for his part, also sent assistance and money, and the Emperor Manuel Comnenus did the same, notwithstanding the fresh discords which had arisen between the courts of Palermo and Byzantium, in consequence of which Sicily drew closer to Venice, who was jealous of Manuel's influence in Ancona, and of the power which that influence gave him in the Adriatic.

Meantime the Pope was attending to his own interests by making much of France, and being very prudent, even yielding, with England, until the murder of Becket assured him an advantage over Henry II. With Manuel, still ambitious of the Western crown, he was extremely courteous, without however compromising himself or giving way in anything, although the Emperor to ingratiate himself with Rome had given a niece of his in marriage to one of the Frangipane. Most of all the Pope trusted in Sicily and in the Lombards, and leant on these last as on his surest support. It was

in Rome that Alexander's authority was weakest, and for
some years he did not reside there, but alternated between
Benevento and some cities of the Campagna, and for a
long time lived at Tusculum, partly to be near Rome,
and partly to preserve that unlucky town from the rage
of the Romans, always intent on its destruction. Neither
was the life of the antipope, Paschal III., a happier one.
The dislike or disdain of the Romans kept him shut
off behind the right bank of the Tiber, but for a short
time only, for on the 20th of September 1168 he died.
His partisans chose for his successor the abbot, John
of Struma, who took the name of Calixtus III.; but the
schism was exhausted, and he was a mere phantom
rival to Alexander. This latter, though hardly master
of his temporal possessions, had acquired on the other
hand a most extensive authority as the henceforth
undisputed spiritual head of the universal Church.

Neither did this fact escape Barbarossa, whose intuition regarding things and men was very clear, even
when he over-estimated his own strength. On his
return from Italy in 1168, he had found Germany in
a troubled state, and had applied himself immediately
with his usual energy to restore order in the kingdom.
The principal promoters of intestine war and feudal
rebellion had been the two most powerful men in Germany, the Saxon Henry the Lion and the northern Margrave, Albert the Bear, who were at mortal enmity.
Frederick did all he could to pacify them, though
inclined to favour Henry on account of old friendship,
and because he hoped to be supported by him in his
plans. But, notwithstanding this hope, he felt the
need of strengthening and providing for himself and

his house against the overweening power of the principal barons. Hence, in April 1169, he obtained the election of his son Henry as King of the Romans, and had him crowned at Aix-la-Chapelle in August by the new archbishop, Philip of Cologne. To his brother Conrad he gave the Palatinate of the Rhine, and recovered for his family the duchy of Suabia, left vacant by the death of Frederick of Rotenburg, whose allodial possessions he also added to his own. He provided for his other son, and, profiting by the hesitation of Henry the Lion, who aspired to the succession but was unwilling to pay for it, he bought at a high price from the prodigal old Duke Guelph VI., who had no direct heirs, the right of succession to his fiefs of Tuscany and Bavaria. This act increased considerably his power both in Italy and Germany, but occasioned him also the enmity of the Saxon Henry.

While thus securing the power of his house and kingdom, Frederick did not forget Italy nor the ecclesiastical problem, which became daily more serious. The protection which he could extend to the antipope, Calixtus III., was insufficient even in Germany, where, at least secretly, the conscience of the clergy was with Alexander. For a moment Frederick hoped to rekindle the schism by gaining over Henry II. of England, but the attempt failed, and he was forced to be cautious, for fear of forfeiting the consent of the barons at the Diet of Bamberg to the election of his son as King of the Romans. He wisely thought of sending an embassy to Alexander III., which, without making any concessions, should raise hopes in Germany of a conciliation with the Church, and at the same time arouse the suspicions of the Lombards and the Sicilian king against the Pope. He chose as messenger the Bishop Eberhard of Bamberg, a man much esteemed for the wise moderation shown by him throughout this controversy. The bishop reached Italy with the power of concluding peace according to his instructions, but under the obligation of not revealing these instructions to any one but the Pontiff himself. The Pope, foreseeing this, and perceiving that the Emperor's object was to sow dissensions between him and the League, had already told the Lombards that he should conclude nothing without them, and had invited them to depute some trusty citizens to be present at his interview with the bishop. Eberhard saw the Pope at Veroli, and insisted on unfolding to him alone the conditions of his mission. These conditions were in reality deceptive. The Emperor demanded that the Pope and his cardinals should recognise the election of his son Henry, and accept as legitimate the schismatic bishops, while he, for his part, would recognise Alexander's ordinations; but as to Alexander himself, he expressed himself vaguely, nor did he state whether he would or would not recognise him as lawful Pope. In the presence of the cardinals and the Lombards Alexander gave his answer. He told Eberhard he wondered at his simplicity in accepting a mission from one so crafty. To recognise his ordinations, and then not to recognise him, Alexander, as Pope, was like worshipping God in part and in part denying Him. His cause had by this time been judged by the whole of God's Church, and by every other king and prince. If Frederick wished to re-enter the Catholic fold, let him bow his head before the Prince of the Apostles. For his part, he was ready to do him honour above every other prince on earth, if he would only show filial affection and maintain the liberty of the Roman Church, which had raised him to the Empire. Thus the good bishop met with no success, and leaving Veroli with a Lombard escort, returned to the Emperor.

The Emperor, meanwhile, having got the princes to elect his son, declared roundly that he would not acknowledge Alexander, and countenanced the antipope, while preparing for another Italian expedition. Having failed in separating the Lombards from the Pope and King of Sicily, there was no choice but to conquer by force of arms, and this without delay, as the League was now paramount in Italy, and even his faithful Pavia had been obliged to give in and join it. Since he could not leave Germany at once, he sent in 1172 an army corps under Christian of Buch, archbishop of Mentz, to engage in political or martial action as occasion demanded, and to serve as a warning to the presumptuous Italians. The warlike archbishop tried to strengthen Genoa's friendly feelings towards the Emperor, and to gain him here and there the goodwill of Tuscany, then proceeded to lay fresh siege to Ancona, with the assistance of ships from Venice, who neglected the interests of the League out of jealousy towards Constantinople. Ancona, though enclosed by land and sea, held out stoutly for six months, and then being succoured by her allies, obliged her enemies to raise the siege and retire.

At length Barbarossa crossed the Alps. He had

with him some princes and bishops, but far fewer than on the former occasion, and Henry the Lion was not among them. Mindful of the affront suffered, Frederick went to Susa and destroyed it; then descending through Piedmont, moved towards Lombardy. On his way he stopped before Asti, which surrendered. The Marquis of Montferrat, the towns of Alba, Acqui, Pavia, and Como, the Count of Biandrate, encouraged by his presence, deserted the League and joined him again. Frederick marched against the new town of Alessandria. Built in opposition to him, named after his greatest enemy, that city represented to him an injury and an insult. It must be destroyed.

He began the siege, but the Lombards were inured to war, and were resolved to open with a glorious page the history of the city. On the first assaults being repulsed, his determination to conquer grew more obstinate, and he drew in his forces more closely. Alessandria resisted firmly. To increase the difficulties of the siege, there followed a very severe winter, and while the army suffered great hardships, the confederates were collecting their forces in order to fall upon the Emperor and crush him. To divide them, Barbarossa sent Christian of Buch into the Bolognese territory, while he redoubled his efforts to take Alessandria; but these failed to conquer the tenacity of its defenders. When the April of 1175 had arrived, he heard that the allies were about to attack him, and he tried to surprise the town by means of a mine; but it was discovered, and he was repulsed with heavy loss. He was forced then to abandon the enterprise, and he advanced rapidly against the army of the League. The two armies encamped at three miles' distance from each other, in the territory of Pavia, between Casteggio and Voghera, and a battle seemed imminent, when suddenly Frederick and the allies began to treat for peace ; but it is not well known who first proposed it. At any rate, it was in Barbarossa's interest to try to gain time, and not to risk for his exhausted army an encounter with the Lombards. A truce was concluded, and they began seriously to discuss terms, while, on Frederick's invitation, three cardinals joined them to try whether peace could also be made with the Church. The negotiations lasted some months, and ended in nothing, so that unable, perhaps not yet caring, to come to an understanding, both sides again had recourse to arms. The year 1175 passed in unimportant encounters, for Frederick stood on the defensive, in expectation of reinforcements from Germany, where, however, things were not going much to his mind. At last, in the spring of 1176, these reinforcements arrived, but without that one of his barons whom he most desired. Frederick had already betaken himself vainly to Chiavenna for an interview with Henry the Lion, to implore him to join once more the Italian expedition. He gained nothing by it but excuses, a cold refusal, and the regret of feeling that he was losing an old friend, and leaving behind him an ungrateful kinsman ready to turn into a rebel.

Frederick, who had gone to meet the reinforcements, having added them to the troops from Como, marched towards Pavia to join the rest of his army ; but the Lombards, hearing of this, advanced rapidly to bar the

way. They met near Legnano on the 29th of May
1176, and a battle ensued. At first the Gérmans had
the advantage, and their cavalry charge threw the Lombards into disorder, but nothing could break down the
determined resistance of those who guarded the *Carroccio*,
and this handful of heroes saved the wavering fortunes
of the battle. The half-routed troops reformed, and made
a ferocious onslaught on the Germans, who gave way.
In vain Frederick, rushing into the thickest of the
fray, urged on his soldiers with his own example. His
horse was killed, and he was lost sight of in the confused mass of combatants ; the rout was complete, and
terrible the slaughter. "Glorious has been our triumph," wrote the Milanese to Bologna, "infinite the
number of the killed among the enemy, the drowned,
the prisoners. We have in our hands the shield, banner,
cross, and lance of the Emperor, and we found silver
and gold in his coffers, and booty of inestimable value ;
but we do not consider these things ours, but the
common property of the Pope and the Italians. In
the fight Duke Berthold was taken, as also a nephew
of the Empress and a brother of the archbishop of
Cologne ; the other captives are innumerable, and they
are all in custody at Milan."

Having retired to Pavia with the remnant of his
defeated army, Frederick Barbarossa felt that the time
had come to change his policy. His mind had been
inclining towards this for some time, and the unwilling steps he had already made towards a conciliation
show that this feeling had already made itself heard
in his counsels, but had not as yet prevailed. Now a
decision must be come to. Four times he had led

armies into Italy and the Italians were still uncon-
quered. In spite of the greatest efforts, it would be
difficult to beat them, and in the long struggle defeats
had always been serious, while the effects of success
were transitory. The German barons wished for peace
with the Church, were tired and suspicious of Italian
expeditions, and in the meantime dark and threatening clouds were lowering in Germany, owing chiefly to
the ambitious designs of Henry the Lion. The Pope,
universally recognised and influential, was in a position to raise obstacles for him in Europe, and the
imperial crown on the head of an excommunicated
man lost much of its fascination and of the hallowed
ideal of the Empire. He had experienced the enmity
of Sicily without having ever succeeded in carrying his
arms into her territory. Constantinople could cause
him trouble if not danger. He had not a single ally.
In such a state of things, it was better to conclude an
honourable peace instead of holding out for the mere
gratification of his pride, reserving his strength for
other needs and his intellect for more successful paths
by which to attain his object.

After considerable reflection Frederick condescended
to speak of peace. First of all he had recourse to the
Pope, convinced that, if he could come to terms with
him, he would be in a better position to treat with the
Lombards and the King of Sicily. Therefore, in October
1176, he sent to Anagni the archbishops Wichmann
of Magdeburg, Christian of Mentz, Conrad the elected
bishop of Worms, and the protonotary Wortwin, with
full powers to offer and conclude peace. The Pope
received them honourably, and after listening to their

message, answered that he desired nothing more fervently than peace ; but that it must be extended also to his allies, and more especially to the King of Sicily, the Lombards, and the Emperor of Constantinople. To this the ambassadors agreed, but asked that the negotiations might be carried on in secret, so as not to divulge them till they were concluded ; " for," they added, " we know well that both on our side and on yours there are some who hate peace and encourage discord."

This was done, and a minute and careful discussion followed, lasting for a good fortnight owing to the many questions which arose between Church and Empire, and to the many powerful personages involved in the schism, whose interests had to be taken into consideration. At last the general conditions of peace were agreed to. In them Frederick recognised Alexander III. as Pope, restored to the Church whatever possessions he had taken away and the right to appoint the prefect of Rome ; he also promised to every ecclesiastic the restitution of all that the schism had deprived him of. The Empress and King Henry also recognised the Pope, and undertook the same obligations as the Emperor. This latter and King Henry were to enter into a fifteen years' peace with the King of Sicily, and were also to make peace with the Emperor of Constantinople and the other allies of the Pope. Christian of Mentz and Philip of Cologne were to be confirmed in their sees, notwithstanding the schismatic origin of their nomination, but provision would be made for the lawful archbishop of Mentz, Conrad of Wittelsbach, by appointing him to the first vacant archbishopric in Germany. The antipope, Calixtus, should have an abbey, and other ecclesiastics were variously provided for. For his part, the Pope recognised Beatrice, Frederick's wife, as Empress, and their son Henry as King of the Romans, and promised to crown them either in person or by deputy. He made peace with the Emperor, undertook to promulgate it in a council, and to have it confirmed by many nobles belonging to Rome and the Campagna, while the Emperor and his son promised to keep the peace for fifteen years with the King of Sicily and a truce of six years with the Lombards.

Such were the headings of this convention of Anagni. Moreover, as, in order to conclude a definite peace, the presence also of the Lombards and of the Emperor himself was necessary, the Pope promised to betake himself with his cardinals near Lombardy. Bologna was chosen as the seat of the congress. On the 9th of March 1178, Alexander embarked on board Sicilian galleys at Vasto on the Adriatic, accompanied by his cardinals and the Sicilian plenipotentiaries, Roger, Count of Andria, high constable of the kingdom, and Romuald archbishop of Salerno, who has left us a very remarkable account of these events. After some days Alexander landed at Venice, and was received with great pomp by Doge and people. The Emperor, who was near Cesena in Romagna, sent then to beg the Pope to agree to change the seat of the congress. Now that the conditions of peace were settled with the Pope, he wanted to separate him as much as possible from the Lombards, in order to treat with them better, and he mistrusted Bologna, the firm and faithful ally of the League. The

Pope, however, replied that he could decide nothing without the consent of the Lombards, and, in order to communicate more easily with them, he moved to Ferrara.

There the delegates of the League met the Pope and the delegates of Sicily and of the Emperor. The Pope made a speech to the Lombards, magnifying the victories of the Papacy over the Empire, and declaring that it was not the work of man, but a miracle of God, that an old unarmed priest should have been able to resist the fury of the Germans, and, without striking a blow, subdue the power of the Emperor. But, he added, though the Emperor had offered peace to him and the King of Sicily, he had declined to conclude it without them, and on this account had engaged in this fatiguing and perilous journey.

The Lombards replied rather ironically, for the treaty of Anagni had made them suspect that the Pope meant to neglect their interests for those of the Church. They thanked him for having condescended to come. The persecution of the Church by the Emperor was well known to them not by hearsay only, but by personal experience of its severity. They were the first to sustain the imperial fury and attack, and had opposed with their bodies and arms the destruction of Italy and of the Church's liberty. For the honour and safety of the Church, and in spite of endless losses and dangers, they had never listened to or received the Emperor and his schismatics, so that it was merely just that he, the Pontiff, not only should not agree to peace with the Emperor without them, but should not even listen to the proposal of it. They had acted thus repeatedly. As to the discomforts and dangers which the Pope had incurred on his journey, how much greater had been their dangers and discomforts in comparison. Nevertheless they also were anxious for a peace which would not touch the honour of Italy or their own liberty, and they were ready to yield to the Emperor his ancient rights, though determined rather to die gloriously as freemen than to drag on a miserable life in servitude. They were glad to hear that the King of Sicily had also agreed to peace.

When the various mediators had been chosen, and before they could even begin to discuss the different articles, the question as to where the discussion should take place blazed up afresh, for the imperialists would not have Bologna, while the Lombards mistrusted Venice. At length Venice was chosen, on condition that the Emperor should swear not to enter the city without the Pope's consent. The disputes were interminable, minute, and often bitter. The claims of the imperialists were considerable, as was also the tenacity of the Lombards ; one side wanted to save as much as they could of the privileges proclaimed at Roncaglia, the other insisted on maintaining their liberty intact, and on yielding to the Empire nothing beyond the rights conceded to Lothair and Conrad III. Peace with the Lombards ceased to be thought of, and instead a truce for six years was proposed as preliminary to a definite peace. The Emperor from a distance raised difficulties. In order to expedite matters, he was allowed to approach as near as Chioggia, but thence, by exciting a rising in the popular party at Venice, Frederick tried to force the Doge to let him enter the city before the negotia-

tions were concluded. The suspicions of the Lombards
were aroused, and they left the town in anger and
retired to Treviso. The Pope was in a great strait, the
conclusion of peace was again in danger, but it was
rescued by the prompt energy of the Sicilian delegates.
Perceiving that the Doge was wavering for fear of the
popular party, they made with great ostentation their
preparations for departure, had their galleys got ready,
and then reproaching the Doge with not having kept
faith, they threatened to leave, and declared that their
king would have his revenge. The threat was serious,
for it meant that the many Venetians in the kingdom
of Sicily would be probably imprisoned and their goods
confiscated. The popular party lost ground through
the fears of the rest of the town, and the Doge was
enabled to resist. When the Sicilian delegates were
convinced that the Emperor would not be allowed to
enter, they let themselves be persuaded to remain.

After this the negotiations proceeded more rapidly ;
the peace with the Pope was concluded the 23d of July
1177, and a truce of fifteen years with Sicily and of six
with the Lombards. The oath was made in the name
of the Emperor, and immediately the Pope commanded
that the Venetian galleys should go to Chioggia for
Frederick, and bring him to St. Niccolò del Lido, where
he was absolved from the ban of excommunication by
several cardinals, while the schismatic prelates abjured
their errors. Then on the 24th of July the Doge, accompanied by the patriarch of Aquileia, went to the
Lido, and conducted the Emperor from Venice in his
own barge. There, in front of St. Mark's, amidst a
deeply moved crowd, the two champions met after an

indefatigable struggle of eighteen years for an ideal supremacy of the power intrusted to them by God. The moment was full of solemnity. The Emperor, overcome by feelings of reverence at the sight of this venerable old man, threw aside his imperial mantle and prostrated himself before him, but the Pope, in tears, raised and kissed him, and leading him into the church, gave him his benediction. The next day the Pope said mass in St. Mark's, in presence of the Emperor, who, on their leaving the church, held the stirrup and offered to conduct the palfrey; but the Pope regarding this homage as granted, dispensed him from accompanying him to his barge.

On the 1st of August the Emperor went to the Pope's residence, and there the peace was solemnly ratified between the Empire and the Church, and the truce with Sicily and the Lombards. The long struggle was finally ended, and in a council held by the Pope in St. Mark's an anathema was pronounced against every and any one who should try to disturb the peace now concluded. Meanwhile in another interview which the Sicilian delegates had with the Emperor, Romuald of Salerno, while confirming the pacific intentions of his sovereign, suggested that an alliance between the kingdom of Sicily and the Empire would be opportune in the interest especially of the Crusades. The Emperor received the suggestion favourably, and during all their stay in Venice he showed particular courtesy to the Sicilians. Perhaps already his active mind was beginning to form new plans with regard to Southern Italy.

After settling some minor points, among others

that concerning the archbishopric of Salzburg, given
to Conrad of Wittelsbach in return for renouncing the
see of Mentz, the Emperor and the Pope separated
about the middle of September.   The first, after some
stay in Central Italy and Lombardy, recrossed the
Alps towards the end of 1177.   Alexander returned
first to Anagni, and then decided to betake himself
to Rome.   The Romans received with great enthusiasm
the successful Pontiff, who after so many storms had
at last steered into port the bark of the Church, but
this enthusiasm was of short duration.   The temporal
power of the Pope was opposed to the independence
of the municipality, and no real harmony between them
was possible.   By the treaty of Anagni the right of
investing the urban prefect had been again secured
to the Pope; but the present one, refusing to pay
homage, retired to Viterbo, and with the assistance of
the Romans continued to countenance the antipope,
who still held out.   The archbishop of Mentz, left in
Italy by Barbarossa, tried in vain to reduce him and
the Romans to obedience.   Alexander, thanks to
his prudence, was more successful; by temporising he
induced the prefect to do him homage, so that the
antipope, deprived of every support, came a sup-
pliant to him at Tusculum.   Alexander received him
affectionately and provided generously for his future.
Another antipope, raised up by the barons of the Campagna, lingered for a few months with the name of
Innocent, but was taken prisoner and shut up in the
abbey of Cava.

After so prolonged a schism and so tangled a chain
of events, it seemed desirable to provide for the fellow-

ship of souls and the peace of the Church. A general council, called by Alexander, met in the Lateran, with a great concourse of bishops and prelates from all quarters. The ordinances of the antipopes were annulled, and among the canons sanctioned was one regarding the election of the Popes, calculated to diminish, if not remove, the possibility of future schism, by establishing that two-thirds of the votes should suffice for a valid election, and where even two-thirds could not agree, then a simple majority should be enough. And this council was the last striking event in the long pontificate of Alexander III., whose life closed two years later at Civita Castellana. He was one of the most remarkable Popes in history, though his genius was not so lofty as that of Gregory VII., who a century before had in great part prepared the way for him. For twenty-two years he guided the Church amid a thousand storms, and in an age of exceptional difficulty. In the ever-renewed struggle between priesthood and Empire, he had for his opponent an emperor of powerful genius and position, whom he overcame. Elected with difficulty against the wish of influential adversaries, under the cloud of bitter schisms which for a long time held all Europe in doubt, he never hesitated nor gave way in a single point. As tenacious as Hadrian IV. in all concerning the great interests of the Church, but more yielding in minor matters, he was sometimes taxed with this pliancy, especially by the partisans of Thomas Becket, and at the time of the peace of Venice by the Lombards; but this reproach was not free from unfairness. An exile from the day that he assumed the tiara, living

C. H.   G

in exile the greater part of his pontificate, he nevertheless witnessed the triumph of the Church. Amidst the thousand details and daily expedients of an arduous policy, he never lost sight of the ideal which inspired him—the supremacy of the Church—just as his greatest adversary was animated by a different ideal, and found in it the source of his strength. This champion of the Church, and the champion of the Empire who stood against him, suggest to the student of history, as he muses on their destinies, that there only where the flame of a high ideal glows in the hearts of men can we hope to find the traces of true greatness.

CHAPTER VII.

(1181–1198.)

*LAST YEARS OF FREDERICK I. — THE EMPEROR
    HENRY VI. AND THE PAPACY—THE CONQUEST
    OF SICILY.*

ALEXANDER'S successor found a question still open between the Church and the Empire, that of the inheritance of the Countess Matilda, which had been left
unsettled at Venice. To avoid its becoming a fresh
cause of discord, the new Pope, Lucius III., had the
delicate task of keeping watch over it, while other
difficulties met him on the threshold of his pontificate.
The Romans especially troubled his peace with their
municipal government and desires for an independent
political life, which found a continual hindrance in the
Papacy, and were also a continual hindrance to it.
Lucius only remained a few months in Rome. He
soon retired to Velletri, and lived for some years here
and there in the Campagna, always on bad terms with
the Romans, who never ceased to threaten Tusculum,
to which Papal protection offered still some sort of
defence. Lucius even resorted for assistance for Tusculum to Christian of Mentz, whose dreaded name and
fierce soldiery held the Romans at a respectful distance

for some time; but the warlike archbishop fell a victim
to the Campagna fever, and died (August 25, 1183),
assisted and blessed by the Pope, whose champion he
had become after having fought against the Church
for so many years.

The Romans growing more daring, the harassed
Pope went into exile at Verona. He went there with
the wish to draw back to the Church the Lombards,
who were seriously estranged, and to treat personally
with Frederick regarding those matters still pending
with the Empire. After the peace of Venice Frederick
had turned all his attention to German affairs, which
were again disturbed, and had carried on a fierce and
successful war against Henry the Lion, who had openly
rebelled. In the November of 1181, at Erfurt, the
vanquished Henry prostrated himself at Frederick's
feet, and then went for some years as an exile to
England, to the court of his father-in-law, Henry II.
Meanwhile a definite peace was in treaty between
Frederick and the Lombards. By this time Frederick
had realised what a power of resistance those republicans possessed, how dangerous was their enmity,
whereas their friendship might be useful. On the
other hand, the Lombards, irritated by the Pope at
Venice, seeing Sicily at peace with Frederick, and
having no hope of help from Constantinople, had no
longer any grounds for fighting, if they could secure
their liberties. This being the feeling on both sides,
peace was treated first at Piacenza, and then concluded at Constance, in a large meeting held there the
25th of June 1183. The conditions were fair. To
the Empire was left unquestioned its high and some-

what ideal sovereignty, and its ancient rights were recognised, but were so limited as not to interfere with the freedom of the republics, or with their development. In accordance with the claims of the Lombards before the battle of Legnano, these rights became again what they were in the time of Henry V. The cities were allowed to have their own consuls and *podestà*, who should administer justice according to their laws; they could also raise new taxes without the Emperor's being able to prevent them, though there would be a right of appeal to him; they were to enjoy all their ancient customs. The Emperor would not require money from the allies who could maintain fortified towns and castles, but with special conditions regarding Crema and Cremona. The right of maintaining the League was untouched, even if necessary of renewing it against the Emperor, and untouched also the right of remaining united to the Church; all offences were mutually forgiven, prisoners exchanged, bans, confiscations, and all other penalties annulled, and the city of Alessandria was respected, but its name changed to Cesarea. Thus did the imperial claims put forward at Roncaglia vanish at Constance, and such was the amicable conclusion to this obstinate struggle between a proud prince, jealous of his rights, and a people determined to resist tyranny. At length a real peace reigned between Frederick and the Lombards of the League.

With the German rebellion subdued and Italy at peace, Frederick Barbarossa could enjoy the proud satisfaction of having done great things during his reign, and of having raised the Empire, through good

fortunes and through bad, to a height not reached for
ages. To celebrate the termination of so many vicissitudes, Frederick commanded a great festival to be held
at Mentz for the Pentecost of 1184. From all sides
princes and commons flocked to it, and as the greatest
ever held before in Germany, it remained celebrated in
the Minnesängers' songs and in popular legends. There,
in a tournament, in which the Emperor himself gave
proofs of his old skill in arms, his son, the young king
Henry VI., won his spurs, and henceforth we find him
taking an active part in the historical drama. After
this, Frederick returned to Italy without an army, sure
this time of a cordial reception from the Lombards.
He wanted to come to a clear understanding with
them, and obtain from the Pope during his lifetime the
imperial crown for his son Henry. But in their meeting at Verona Pope and Emperor soon felt that the
causes of discord had not been all removed at Venice,
and that new ones might spring up easily. The Emperor insisted that the Pope should confirm the orders
already conferred by the schismatic bishops, but the
Pope, after brief hesitation, said he could not make
this concession without a council, which, however, he
promised to convoke shortly at Lyons. This refusal
displeased Frederick, and rendered it a delicate matter
to treat concerning the possessions of the Countess
Matilda, with respect to which, moreover, neither of
the two sides seemed disposed to yield, the one insisting on the inherent right of succession of the Emperor,
and the other maintaining that derived from the famous
donation made by Matilda. Thus the question dragged
on without coming nearer to a conclusion, and in the

meantime Frederick held these possessions and had no intention of giving them up. A third ground of discord came from the archbishopric of Trier, where, in 1183, a double election had occurred, and while the Pope favoured Folmar, one of the two elected, the Emperor supported the other. Finally, Frederick persistently demanded the imperial crown for Henry, but Lucius was decided in his refusal, alleging that the co-existence of two emperors was incompatible with the very nature of the Empire, and that Frederick must needs first resign the crown if he wished to place it on his son's head. Things were in this insecure state when, on the 24th of November 1185, Lucius III. died at Verona. Lambert Crivelli, archbishop of Milan, immediately succeeded him under the name of Urban III. He had no love for Frederick, and was a haughty and energetic man, from whom little concession was to be expected.

Meanwhile the Emperor, seeing how little he could hope for lasting peace with the Popes, had turned his attention to undermining and isolating them. On that account he flattered the Lombards, and especially reconciled himself so far with the Milanese as to allow Crema to rise again from her ruins and unite with them against Cremona. Nor was this all; for he secretly was labouring towards the accomplishment of a greater plan. There was no longer any hope that William II. of Sicily would have offspring; and since the constitution of the kingdom did not exclude women from the throne, Constance, daughter of Roger and aunt of William, might be considered the heir-presumptive. Frederick asked the hand of this princess for his son Henry, and the marriage was concluded rapidly, notwithstanding all the efforts of the Pope, on whom the unexpected news fell like a thunderbolt. In spite of a strong party, which foresaw and opposed in this alliance the ruin of Norman rule in Sicily, the barons of the realm swore to recognise Constance and her husband as William II.'s heirs. In this way Frederick at last reached Sicily, surrounded the Papal territory, and, by enlarging the borders of the Empire, was approaching the Bosphorus. In great pomp the bride crossed Italy and reached Milan, where the marriage was celebrated. Constance was thirty-one, eight years older than her husband, and apparently of a very different disposition; but nothing else was considered but the high political value of the alliance, which was concluded with great pomp and splendour. Frederick wished that his son should then assume the iron crown, and that Constance also should be crowned as queen. It belonged to Urban, who had reserved for himself the see of Milan, to crown the new king of Italy; but he refused, and Frederick, without hesitation, had his son crowned by the patriarch of Aquileia and the queen by another bishop. The wrath of the Pontiff at this imperial indifference found vent in the excommunication of the bishops who had taken part in the ceremony; and shortly afterwards, cutting short the controversy still pending, he made Folmar a cardinal and consecrated him bishop of Trier.

Pope and Emperor were again at open war. Urban, by blaming seriously the conduct of the Emperor, tried with some success to win over the principal German prelates, so that Frederick thought it prudent to remedy this evil by returning to Germany, leaving his son behind him to keep the Pope in check. Henry proved himself no timid follower of his father, and not only by holding out firmly with regard to the Countess Matilda's possessions and other controverted matters, but in many other partial acts showed a resolution bordering on arrogance and tending to despotism. It is said that he commanded his servants to roll in the mud one bishop who had dared to declare to his face that he held his investiture from the Pope. By occupying Tuscia and introducing his troops into the Church territory, he prevented any communication between Rome and the Pope at Verona, against whom he also closed the passes of the Alps. And so determined was he to isolate the Pope, that once, on the arrest of a messenger who was carrying money to Urban, he had his nose cut off, and without ceremony appropriated the money.

Frederick in the meantime had assembled the German bishops, and by expounding the causes of the new disagreement won over to his side all except Philip, archbishop of Cologne, who frankly declared to him that he considered him in the wrong. The bishops wrote to the Pope recommending moderation. The Pope, grieved by their unexpected desertion, wrote to the Emperor justifying himself, and making fresh complaints against him and against Henry's violent conduct. The situation became embittered, and Urban was preparing to excommunicate Frederick, when he died at Ferrara on the 20th of October 1187. It would have been difficult even for the most conciliatory successor of Urban to have avoided a conflict with

the Empire; but a terrible piece of news averted the
storm, by directing elsewhere the thoughts and fears
of Christendom. Jerusalem had fallen into the hands
of Saladin, and the Holy Sepulchre was again polluted
by Mussulman hordes.

The news filled with consternation the whole of
Europe, accustomed for a century to look towards
Jerusalem as the ideal goal of all her aspirations.
The sleeping echoes of Peter the Hermit's and St.
Bernard's words seemed to reawaken, and the old cry
calling on Christians to take up the cross was again
heard. Gregory VIII. (Urban's successor), during
his two months' pontificate, and after him Clement
III., showed themselves peacefully disposed towards
the Empire, and concentrated all their efforts in drawing people and princes to the crusade. They were
fairly successful. While the kings of France and
England took the cross, Pope and Emperor were
trying to clear away the misunderstandings existing
between them. For a moment the inheritance of
Matilda seemed forgotten, and the question of Trier
took a turn satisfactory to the Emperor. Henry,
recognised now as *Emperor-elect*, whose coronation
would take place some day, had relaxed his rigour and
raised the kind of blockade endured by Urban III.
Thus Gregory VIII. had been able to betake himself
to Pisa, to reconcile the Pisans and Genoese in order
that their ships might act in concert for the recovery
of the Holy Land; and Clement III., as soon as
elected, feeling perhaps the necessity of again putting
foot in Rome, had come to terms with the Roman
republic by implicitly recognising its rule, and in the

beginning of 1188 had re-entered the city. The principal condition of this agreement with the Roman people was the destruction of Tusculum, in which the Pope had to concur.

As pontifical legate for declaring the crusade in France and Germany went the cardinal Henry of Albano, who at Mentz had a colloquy with Frederick, and while on the one side he tried to give an amicable termination to the controversies arisen during the stormy pontificate of Urban, he forwarded, on the other hand, the interests of the great undertaking he had to proclaim. Frederick, with his chivalrous spirit and his thirst for glory, could not remain indifferent when from every breast came the cry for rescue, and the flower of European knighthood on the point of starting for Jerusalem were awaiting their leader. The Empire had now reached that summit of glory of which Frederick had dreamed when the crown was placed on his head amidst the triumphant shouts of his Germans and the clashing arms of the infuriated and rebellious Romans. The destinies of his house were assured, and were not likely to fail in the resolute grasp of his son Henry. For thirty years, amid endless anxieties, dangers, and fatigues, the glory of his name had spread from the remote north to the prosperous south, and the reign of Frederick in strength of arms and power of law perhaps equalled— certainly was not far from equalling—the reigns of Charlemagne and Otto. In Europe, his work was accomplished, but there remained for him elsewhere an enterprise such as no other Emperor had undertaken, and which might crown his life's work by raising it to a point of glory never reached before. Neither Charlemagne nor Otto at the end of their career had had the opportunity or the power to free the sepulchre of Christ from the pollution of the infidel hordes, but to him, the favourite of fortune, the opportunity was offered and he felt himself equal to seizing it.

From the hands of the cardinal Henry Frederick took the cross, and doubtless in that hour there returned to his mind memories of the time when, about forty years before, he, a youth, had received the cross from St. Bernard, and had gone to meet his first dangers and win his first laurels. Before starting he showed his experience in war and statescraft by preparing everything for the expedition with great care, and by putting the affairs of the Empire in order, reconciling dissensions between various German princes, making peace with the archbishop of Cologne, and sending Henry the Lion away from Germany for three years in the hope of avoiding disturbances. At Regensburg in the spring of 1189 the fine and powerful army of crusaders collected, and Frederick, taking the command, marched towards the East, accompanied by his son Frederick, Duke of Suabia.

There remained behind in Europe King Henry VI., whose hand thenceforth held the reins of government in Germany and Italy. Henry inherited from his father a tenacious disposition and an unlimited ambition. More cultivated than his father and with many statesmanlike qualities, he did not equal him in his military genius nor in that fertility of expedients which was one of Frederick's greatest gifts. Like his father, he was violent, but he was more cruel, and had none of those generous instincts and of that ideality of mind which from his youth had gained for Frederick the admiration even of his enemies. Frederick, a man of real greatness, identified himself with the abstract idea of the Empire, and fusing it with his own personal ambition, fondly exaggerated its power. Henry, on the contrary, made use of this idea for his personal grandeur, for which he specially laboured with a greedy unscrupulous ambition, with untiring ardour, and unflinching persistence.

Hardly was Frederick gone when countless occasions for trying his strength presented themselves to the young King of the Romans. Henry the Lion had quickly availed himself of the Emperor's absence to return to Germany, where he regained a part of his states by force or by the aid of revolts. At that moment William the Good died at Palermo, and Henry VI. and his wife Constance found themselves heirs to the kingdom of Sicily. It was necessary to return in all haste to Italy to take possession of that kingdom before the latent disaffection among the barons should break out openly and increase the hindrances to a change of dynasty. Therefore, after adopting wise and vigorous measures to reduce Henry the Lion to terms, the young king applied himself to preparing an Italian expedition, but was not in time to prevent the difficulties which arose in Sicily. There the people, grown attached to the Norman dynasty of the Hauteville, did not like the idea of being subject to a new foreigner, and this also displeased many barons, who foresaw a loss of influence consequent on that which would be gained by the Germans whom Henry would bring with him. Party feeling increased, and the Pope, alarmed at the idea of being enclosed in a sort of cage between the power of Henry to south as well as north, encouraged the opposition, which grew and spread so rapidly that in the January of 1190, without any regard for the hereditary rights of Constance, a new king, also of the blood of the Hauteville, was elected, namely, Tancred, Count of Lecce, the illegitimate son of a brother of Constance. After a brief hesitation Tancred took the crown at Palermo, and the Pope immediately gave him the investiture of the kingdom.

By this act the Pope placed his relations with Henry VI. on a very difficult footing, but they were both interested in not coming to an open rupture, and dissimulated mutually their latent and hostile suspicions. Having patched up matters with Henry the Lion, the king now found himself otherwise entangled in Germany, and had to try not to add ecclesiastical difficulties to the many opposing him both there and in Italy, whither he wished to proceed without delay. Then suddenly came an announcement which spread like wildfire through the whole of Europe, and increased Henry's need for caution in his dealings with the Pope. The great Frederick Barbarossa, the glorious Emperor, was dead. Far, far away in distant Asia, after overcoming vast difficulties and perils innumerable, he was drowned in a river in Seleucia on the 10th of June 1189, while leading on his army through those dreary wastes amidst enemies constantly repulsed and as constantly swarming anew to the attack. Such was his end, and his country saw him no more, while his bones lie in an unknown spot beside those of his son Frederick of Suabia in the desert sands of Antioch. But the love of Germany, breathing in fantastic legends, planted her hero's resting-place high aloft in the Thuringian cliffs, and there she would have him lie bound in magic slumber to await the call that should arouse him to lead her armies anew to victory.

The death of Frederick rendered it more urgent for his successor to betake himself to Italy and to avoid unpleasantness with the Pope, from whom he had now to ask the imperial crown. In the November of 1190, Henry crossed the Alps and began to treat with the Romans and the Pope for the coronation, while he sought by flattery and promises to secure the co-operation of Pisa and Genoa for the conquest of Naples and Sicily. There the new king, Tancred, was meeting with many difficulties. Party feeling had flared up. A strong nucleus of barons, urged on by Walter Offamil, the archbishop of Palermo, had taken up arms in favour of Constance and Henry. Tancred had, therefore, been obliged to fight against this revolt as also against the troops sent into the kingdom by Henry VI. while still in Germany. Moreover, the King of France, Philip Augustus, and the English Richard the Lion-hearted had caused him serious embarrassments when they touched at Sicily on their way to the crusades.

Clement III. dreaded Henry's coming to Rome, where the young king was winning over the Romans by asking from them as much as from him the crown of the Empire, recognising a claim of theirs which his father had always proudly denied. Henry was conforming to the needs of the moment. The Roman republic was now so strong that the Pope was weak before it, and in his heart he was hostile to Henry, who flattered the Romans in order to wrest from him a speedy consent to the coronation. The Pope had neither means nor pretext for resistance, and the ceremony was fixed for the Easter of 1191, when, a few weeks before, Clement died, and on his successor, Celestine III., devolved the ungrateful duty of the coronation. While Henry was advancing, the Romans, seizing the favourable occasion, offered to overcome the Pope's hesitation on condition that Henry would hand over to the Pope, and the Pope to them, Tusculum, which was still standing. The cruel bargain was struck, and Tusculum was sacrificed to the brutal hatred of Rome. The coronation of Frederick I. had cost the life of Arnold of Brescia, and now Tusculum paid with the blood of her defenceless citizens the price of Henry's crown. On the 14th of April 1191, while the German sovereign was at the gates, Celestine III. was himself ordained Pope, and the following day he placed the imperial crown on the heads of Henry and Constance,—a sinister beginning to the feeble pontificate of the aged Celestine, forced to crown an Emperor who was advancing towards an enterprise involving the Papacy in danger, and to abandon to the ferocity of a people whom the Popes could no longer restrain an unfortunate city which they had not been able to protect. Perhaps this very feebleness is the reason why the relations between Church and Empire offer so little interest during the lives of Celestine and Henry.

Immediately after his coronation, Henry, turning a deaf ear to the Pope's entreaties, started on the expedition for Naples, accompanied by the Empress as heiress of the realm. The first moves were fortunate, in spite of the valour of the Count of Acerra, Tancred's brother-in-law, who encountered the imperial army. Tancred, instead of advancing against his enemies, was occupied in celebrating with feasts and rejoicings the marriage of Irene, daughter of the Emperor of Constantinople, to his eldest son, Roger, to whom on that occasion he gave the title of king. Not so had the first Normans conquered and held the kingdom; nor was it so that he could hope to repulse his resolute antagonist, who, rapidly reaching Naples, found the city determined on resistance, and began a siege.

This siege for the time was unlucky for Henry. While the promised assistance of Pisan and Genoese ships was delayed, and the city, free on her seaboard, was being abundantly victualled, the imperial army was in want of everything. Summer coming on, there were added to this extreme need and to the attacks of the besieged also epidemic fevers, which consumed the Germans terribly. He reiterated his entreaties and promises to Pisa and Genoa, in hopes of hastening them, promising, among other things, to the Genoese the possession of Syracuse as soon as Sicily was in his power. Pisans and Genoese arrived, but too late, and being held at bay by the strong Sicilian fleet under the admiral Margarito, were powerless to help. Meanwhile sickness was raging among the imperial troops. Conrad of Bohemia and the archbishop of Cologne succumbed to fever, and the Emperor himself fell ill. There was no alternative but to raise the siege and retire (August 24, 1191). Tancred could easily have cut off Henry's retreat and exterminated him, but he remained inactive at Messina, and the opportunity was lost.

The Empress Constance had, however, become his prisoner. The people of Salerno, after first receiving her with great honour, when they saw Henry's cause in danger, stopped her and sent her as a valuable hostage to Palermo. Tancred entertained his noble prisoner with great courtesy, and consigned her to the affectionate care of his wife, Sibilla, who was later to be ill repaid for her kindness. Henry, meanwhile, after placing a garrison here and there, left the kingdom, went first to Genoa, where he solemnly renewed his promise of concessions in return for their promise of assistance, and then entered Lombardy, where he remained till towards the end of the year. There all the old discords were breaking out afresh among the cities, nor did the presence of the Emperor serve to soothe them; indeed, the favours granted by him to Cremona aroused the wrath of Milan and other cities, which were already beginning to regard him as an enemy. Towards the end of the year he returned to Germany to attend to the new insurrection of the Guelph party led by Henry the Lion, and at the same time appealed to the Pope to obtain the Empress's freedom. The Pope, who shortly before had placed the monastery of Monte Cassino under an interdict on account of its fidelity to the Emperor, now, with a weak and vacillating policy, listened to Henry's appeal, and sent a cardinal to Palermo. The unwary Tancred liberated Constance, and sent her back without ransom and enriched with precious gifts. Neither Tancred nor the Pope obtained what they hoped for by their compliance, and neither Henry nor even Constance appear to have been touched by it. Henry paid no attention to entreaties coming from Rome for a reconciliation with Tancred, and in the spring of 1192, Roffrid, abbot of Monte Cassino, on his return from Germany with a few soldiers, put heart into the imperialists left behind in the kingdom, who were able to drag on the war till the return of the Emperor.

This return met with many difficulties, chief among which was that of money; but to Henry, lucky and unscrupulous, a strange opportunity presented itself for obtaining money, nor was he restrained by the wickedness of the means or the fear of dishonour. On his way home from Palestine, Richard the Lion-hearted had fallen into the hands of Leopold, Duke of Austria, and the Emperor, seizing this occasion, gained possession of his person and kept him prisoner in the castle of Trifels. False pretexts and accusations against Richard failed to justify an act of such miscreant ruffianism, but Henry cared little for that. Nor did he attend to the prayers and menaces of the Pope, who in vain demanded that the royal crusader should be set at liberty, and later, by excommunicating Leopold of Austria and his accomplices, included by implication the Emperor. Richard at length regained his liberty in February 1194, but at the price of that gold which was destined to work the destruction of the Norman monarchy in Sicily.

The war which Henry now conducted in Southern Italy was very successful. Tancred and his eldest son, Roger, were already dead. The kingdom had passed to the boy William, under the regency of Queen Sibilla, and their insecure position deprived them of supporters. Henry entered the realm after ensuring the co-operation of Genoa and Pisa by repeating solemn promises to hand over to them all the principal maritime cities in the two Sicilies. He advanced rapidly, and met with few obstacles. He avenged with ferocity at Salerno the seizure of Constance, filled with terror and slaughter the places he suspected of fidelity to the Normans, and made much of those which came spontaneously to him. In a short time nearly all the mainland belonging to the kingdom was taken. The ships of Genoa and Pisa, under the command of the great seneschal of the Empire, Markwald, appeared before Messina, which surrendered to Henry, as did Palermo shortly after. Queen Sibilla, who with her son had taken refuge in the castle of Calatabellotta, also gave herself up under conditions destined later to be broken, and the boy William laid down his crown at the feet of Henry. Towards the chief barons of the realm the Emperor at that time showed indulgence, notwithstanding their revolt; nay, he loaded them with honours and titles. On the 20th of November 1194 he made a triumphal entry into Palermo, and was crowned at Christmas amidst great rejoicings. After so many troubles the people breathed more freely, hoping that the long years of blood and suffering were over; but the respite was brief.

The day after the coronation, the Empress, who was on her way to rejoin Henry, on arriving at Iesi in the Marche, on the 26th of December 1194 gave birth to a boy, who received the names of his grandfathers, Frederick and Roger. Great was the Emperor's delight, and since everything was now succeeding with him, he felt encouraged to mature still wider plans of universal dominion. But first he wished to rid himself of those Norman barons to whom, shortly before, he had been lavish of gifts and honours. As a pretext for this, he made use of a conspiracy, real or pretended, which he stifled in blood, and the chief men of the realm either perished on the scaffold, or, like the admiral Margarito and the archbishop of Salerno, were left to die in dark dungeons. Tancred's unfortunate young son, after being blinded and mutilated, was sent to Germany, where also his sisters and mother found a convent-prison. The bodies of Tancred and his son Roger were removed from the royal tomb, as unworthy of resting among the lawful lords of a realm they had usurped. Only the Greek princess Irene, the childless widow of Roger, found favour in Henry's eyes, and he gave her in marriage to his brother Philip. Probably in allying his family with that of Constantinople he was providing for those plans which from Palermo he was naturally led to widen and enlarge.

Henry's good luck, resolution, and rapidity had, as it were, paralysed the Pontiff in presence of the conquest of a kingdom to the suzerainty of which he also laid claim. For some time Celestine maintained a sort of sulky silence; then, when the Emperor began to make overtures, he sent him some cardinals, but they concluded nothing, and the relations between them were reduced to the querulous complaints of a powerless old man, listened to with indifference by the disdainful young sovereign. Nevertheless this latter avoided an open rupture. Since he had no reason to fear the Pope, it was useless to drive him to extremes, the more so as among his plans were some for which papal co-operation would be serviceable. In the spring of 1195 he started for Germany, stopping on his way at Pavia, but without result, as the Lombards were again unquiet, and many of them hostile to the Empire. At Pavia the Genoese presented themselves to ask for the fulfilment of the conditions agreed to touching the conquest of Sicily; but Henry repulsed them, and openly declared his intention of not keeping his promises. Nor were the Pisans more fortunate, and the two cities saw too late the trap into which the astute and disloyal Emperor had enticed them.

On his return to Germany, Henry tried to carry out his design of changing the constitution of the Empire and making it hereditary in his family. Various discords which had troubled Germany during his absence were dying out, and the great representative of the Guelph family, Henry the Lion, died at that time. Everything seemed favourable. The Emperor made great efforts to persuade the German nobility to accept this change, alleging the state of disorder into which Germany was thrown by each fresh election, and offering to modify very greatly in favour of their families the feudal constitution. He also tried to gain over Celestine, who as usual vacillated, appearing favourable for a moment, then retracting and declaring himself opposed to it. And indeed no Pope could have approved of a change which would have deprived the Church of every hold on the Empire, by destroying implicitly the political importance of the consecration and coronation. All Henry's efforts were in vain, and the constitution of the Empire remained unchanged.

Henry, when he saw the impossibility of this, changed his tactics in order to reach his end, at least in part. He asked that his son Frederick, who was less than two years old and not yet baptized, should be elected King of the Romans, and this was done. In the meantime there was a movement in favour of a fresh expedition to Palestine, which he encouraged, organising a strong band of crusaders, and hinting that he would himself somewhat later take the Cross. With this he flattered the Pope, diverted the thoughts of the Germans from their dissensions, and made use of it to prepare an army which might partly pass through his kingdom and help him to wipe out the last traces of resistance. The Empress was then ruling the kingdom from Palermo, but it does not appear that she enjoyed Henry's confidence, suspicious as he was lest the Norman sympathies natural in her might prevail. In July 1196 Henry returned to Italy, and till September remained in Lombardy, then proceeded to the south, and stayed some months at Capua, where, to the continual complaints of the Pope on many controversial points, he replied by treating with him at great length, but without ever coming to any conclusion. There the brother-in-law of Tancred fell into his hands, that Richard, Count of Acerra, who had first raised arms against him, and who was accused, moreover, of many other serious offences. Condemned to death, Richard was first dragged at a horse's tail, then hung up still living by the feet to a gallows. Two days later Henry's jester tied a stone to his throat, and thus strangled, the victim was released from his horrible sufferings.

From Capua Henry passed over to Palermo. He had, in the meantime, obtained by threats from the Emperor of Constantinople a rich tribute and promises of forage and transports for his crusaders. Thus his power spread, and perhaps his secret ambition aimed at uniting on his head the crowns of the two Empires. But in the Sicilian kingdom, oppressed and overtaxed, the leaven of discontent was still fermenting, and he set himself to destroy it. A fresh conspiracy was discovered, and blood again flooded the scaffolds, and new and horrible tortures spread terror and execration till the end of the summer of 1197. At that time Henry, while hunting in a forest not far from Messina, was seized with sudden malaric fever, from which he died in a few days, leaving in his place the child Frederick II. under the guardianship of his mother. Thus the career of Henry VI. was unexpectedly cut short. He had received from his father a great inheritance, and he had held and enlarged it with the paternal

tenacity, but without a ray of that magnanimity of
soul which shone forth in Barbarossa. He was as
fortunate as he was perfidious, and he died young
enough not to see his luck turn, for he was not the
man to have commanded good fortune for the space
of a long life. He had succeeded to the reins of
government in a propitious hour, and had lived for
that hour only, when the majesty of the Empire was
at its height, Germany tired of her dissensions, the
Lombards sufficiently pacified, Sicily torn with internal discords, the Papacy in aged and infirm hands.
But when he died, the power of the Church was
about to pass into very different keeping. On the 8th
of January 1198, Pope Celestine also died, and Innocent III. was elected in his stead.

CHAPTER VIII.

(1198–1201)

INNOCENT III. GUARDIAN OF FREDERICK II., KING
OF SICILY — HIS STRUGGLE WITH PHILIP OF
HOHENSTAUFEN.

THE new Pope ascended the papal throne with a great
faith in the supremacy of the Papacy over every
earthly power, and with a firm determination to
make it triumph. Issuing from the noble Roman
stock of the Conti, he had been created cardinal very
early by his maternal uncle, Clement III., but during
the pontificate of Celestine, who was unfriendly to
his family, he had remained in the background, and
occupied more with thought and study than with
action. A young man of thirty-seven, he had a
high reputation for learning on jurisprudence, acquired in the schools of Paris and Bologna; his
appearance was noble, his life pure, his will active
and tenacious. He was of affable manners, but
prone to sudden anger, and also inclined to that
melancholy not uncommon to thoughtful minds,
which had led to his writing a book, already famous,
on the contempt of the world.

The feeble rule of Celestine and the resolute

policy of Henry VI. had endangered the interests
of the Church. It was necessary to strengthen them,
and, by continuing and completing the work of
Gregory VII. and of Alexander III., finally place the
Papacy on the summit of its power. To realise
this vast idea, it would be necessary for Innocent to
embrace in his view the whole of Christendom; but
first of all he had to provide for nearer and immediate needs. The temporal power of the Church
was almost destroyed, not only in Rome, where the
authority of the republic prevailed, but throughout
the Church's patrimony, which Henry had parcelled
out among the German barons who had accompanied
him. But the edifice built up by Henry was already
crumbling, and Innocent soon obtained that the
prefect of Rome should receive the investiture from
him, thus converting him from an imperial into a
papal officer, while, without interfering with the
autonomy of the republic and senate, he prevailed
on them to recognise explicitly his sovereign authority
over Rome.

On the death of Henry VI. the latent hatred of
the oppressive German rule broke out fiercely and
openly. Philip of Suabia, Henry's brother, had
escaped with difficulty from the possessions of Countess Matilda, held by him under the title of Duke of
Tuscany, in order to return to Germany and attend
there to the interests of his house. The provinces
of the Exarchate and of the March of Ancona were
in the hands of Markwald of Anweilen, the fiercest
of Henry VI.'s tools, and now head of the German
party in Italy, while the duchy of Spoleto was held

by Conrad of Uerselingen. Aided by the hatred of
the people against the Germans, Innocent succeeded
in wresting from them a great part of their possessions. Conrad of Uerselingen, after having vainly
offered to hold the duchy of Spoleto as a papal
fief, had to leave it and return to Germany. The
Tuscan cities, liberated from the presence of Philip
of Hohenstaufen and assisted by Innocent, raised
the standard of municipal freedom and joined in a
league among themselves, with the exception of the
powerful Pisa, which remained faithful to the imperial cause, and would not pay homage to the
Pope. It was less easy to regain the March of
Ancona, for Markwald made armed resistance; but
at last he also yielded, though only to renew the
struggle on another field. Thus, in a short space
of time, the whole of Central Italy was freed from
the German yoke, and a great part of it accepted
either the immediate or the indirect sovereignty of
the Pontiff, who had done so much to raise and guide
its movements.

Neither was the Teutonic domination less hated in
the south, but rebellion there took other forms. The
Norman Constance, on the death of her husband, seized
the reins of government, and, with the support of the
Norman nobility, deprived the Germans of all power
and excluded them from the land, while her child
Frederick, who had remained in the Marche since his
birth, was brought to her. The high seneschal Markwald, in whose hand was Henry VI.'s will, in vain
laid claim to the tutelage of the boy-king. Hateful
to the Sicilians, and suspected of coveting the throne

of Sicily for himself, he also had to leave the island, and retire first to the county of Molise, and then proceed to defend as best he might his possessions in Romagna and the Marche, which the people in revolt and the Pope were trying to tear away from him. Constance in the meantime, anxious to secure the throne for her son, sought the support of Rome. She turned first to Celestine, then to Innocent, asking again for that investiture of the kingdom which the powerful Henry had scorned. Innocent did not wish to see the two crowns of Sicily and the Empire united on one head, so he temporised prudently, measuring his concessions according to the turn things took in Germany, and putting as first condition the abrogation of the privileges which at the peace of Benevento in 1156 Hadrian IV. had been compelled to concede to William I. Constance tried in vain to persuade the Pope to waive these claims, for he saw the strength of his position and persisted. Having obtained what he wanted, Innocent promised his protection to the Empress, and sent Cardinal Ugolino of Ostia to receive from her liege homage in her own and her son's name. But soon after, in November 1198, Constance died at Palermo. Before her death, with a keen apprehension of the dangers awaiting her son, she thought to defend him by appointing Innocent as regent of Sicily and her son's guardian. She appointed also a council of government which should maintain order till the arrival of the papal legate, and to the very last she charged them to beware of Markwald, and not to make peace with him. Thus her short reign had been entirely a reaction against German influence, and had been sufficient to shake it considerably, if not entirely to eradicate it.

Innocent accepted the guardianship of the boy Frederick, a thorny task for him, who had to watch over the interests of his ward and those of the Church, which were so often opposed to each other. It was to Cardinal Cencius, later Pope Honorius III., that he intrusted the duty of representing him in Sicily and of educating Frederick, and the cardinal immediately surrounded the boy by cultivated men calculated to inspire him with a love of letters. Meanwhile the conditions of the kingdom were growing more and more complicated. As Constance had foreseen on her deathbed, the German party soon lifted its head, supported by the Sicilian Saracens, who were hostile to the Pope, and by the secret plots of Walter Palear, bishop of Troia, one of the councillors of the regency and high chancellor of the kingdom. This man had hoped to have all the power in his hands during Frederick's minority, and bitterly resenting the intrusion of this papal authority, he took to conspiring secretly against it and favouring the spread of discontent. Markwald, now dispossessed of the March of Ancona, tried to recover his position by entering the county of Molise, where were the remnants of his followers, collected an army, and affirmed anew his claims on the guardianship of Frederick and the regency of the kingdom. He sought to draw over to his side Roffrid, abbot of Monte Cassino, whose monastery was a key to the kingdom from its position and the troops of which it disposed. But Roffrid, who had been always devoted to Henry VI., divided the cause of this son from that of Markwald, and was faithful to the oath of homage which he had sworn to Innocent. Markwald cruelly ravaged the monastery's lands, took possession of the town of San Germano, and ascending to the very gates of the convent, laid siege to it. Not succeeding in storming it, he hoped to conquer it by thirst, but a sudden rain falling, as it appeared by miracle, on the day of St. Maurus, destroyed his camp and supplied the besieged with water. Markwald raised the siege, and after getting money out the abbot, retired.

The Pope meanwhile was reiterating anathemas and collecting troops against him. Markwald, feeling the urgency of hastening to Palermo and seizing the government, entered into treaty in order to gain time, and offered to submit to the Pope, who, either because he fell into the trap or from its being difficult to do otherwise, absolved him. It looked like a peace, but was in reality only a truce favourable to Markwald. This latter was to give up every claim, keep away from Sicily, and indemnify Monte Cassino for the losses suffered ; but he kept none of these promises. On the contrary, having secured the assistance of the Saracens and of as many malcontents as Apulia and Sicily contained, he took up arms again, entered Salerno, and thence sailed for the island in the ships of Pisa, which hoped by joining him to over-power Genoese influence in the kingdom. On the mainland he left Diepold, Count of Acerra, to en-counter such troops as the Pope was sure to send against him.

The boy Frederick was taken for safety to Messina,

while the Pope encouraged the people to hold out, and sent a first expedition of troops under the command of a relative and accompanied by some prelates. Meanwhile a Frenchman, Count Walter of Brienne, presented himself to Innocent. He had married Albina, a daughter of King Tancred, and in her name claimed the fiefs of Lecce and Taranto, of which Henry VI. had unjustly deprived her family. She, with her mother Sibilla, had accompanied her husband to Rome. The Pope, after hesitating a little, and fearing to drive him over to the enemy, thought it prudent to respond favourably to the pretensions of this adventurer, and to use him against Markwald. This latter, having seized on a large part of the island, went to attack Palermo; but encountering the Pope's and Frederick's soldiers near the town, met with a serious defeat and was obliged to fly, leaving Henry VI.'s will among the booty of the camp. Not for this, however, did he lose heart. The strength of his adversaries was being frittered away by difficulties and dissensions, and he took advantage of it to remain in Sicily, where he continued to intrigue and to raise soldiers. In this he succeeded. The high chancellor, Walter Palear, who had already been secretly plotting with him, now openly joined him and recalled him to the council of the kingdom; but he soon found that he had raised up a master, and was forced to leave the island, while Markwald seemed about to reach in triumph the goal of his ambition.

Then the Pope set loose upon the kingdom Walter of Brienne with a handful of French knights, to whom were added reinforcements sent by the abbot of Monte Cassino and the Count of Celano. Diepold of Acerra went to meet Walter, but was defeated near Capua, and this opened up Apulia to the Frenchman. A year of great confusion followed in the realm, the mainland being divided between Walter of Brienne and Diepold, while Sicily was in the hands of Markwald, who had at last succeeded in entering Palermo and assuming the guardianship of Frederick. But in September 1202 Markwald fell ill and died, and in Apulia Diepold was again beaten in that same plain of *Cannæ*, where in old days the Romans had suffered their famous defeat. Innocent was rejoiced, thinking that he had now the advantage; but in the ever-recurring civil discords and the ambition of the magnates he met with endless opposition, nor could he, oppressed as he was by a thousand different cares, devote all his attention or all his resources to a single enterprise. The war dragged on, and Diepold was able to surprise Walter of Brienne, who was killed. Innocent, temporising as he best could in the midst of such confusion, managed to maintain pretty well the integrity of the kingdom for his ward, and even partly to draw over to himself those very same ambitious barons who had formerly tried to thwart his plans.

Thus, in a palace that to him was almost a prison, amid discords, suspicions, and snares, Frederick's sad childhood had passed in loveless solitude; and now that he had reached his fourteenth year, he began to wield the sceptre and to govern by himself. But the boy-king's hand was still weak, the kingdom still torn by dissensions, his poverty was great, and his councillors were greedy of power and riches, at variance among themselves and without affection for him. Sicily was still shaken by rebellion and on the mainland Conrad of Marley, another lieutenant of Henry VI.'s, was leading the German forces, and was acting as master on his own account in the Abruzzi and the Terra di Lavoro. Innocent came to the assistance of the king, and, raising an army, intrusted the command of it to his brother, Richard, Count of Segni, who entered the Terra di Lavoro, and, supported by the faithful abbot Roffrid of Monte Cassino and by the Count of Celano, entirely defeated Conrad and destroyed the influence of the German barons in that district. Innocent then resolved upon going in person to reinforce the royal authority. In Rome, after a troubled period of conflict and agitation, people's minds had calmed down, so that Innocent could leave the city, and passing through Anagni and Ceprano, entered the kingdom on the 21st of June 1208. Received with great honour by all, his presence was admirably calculated to restore order and heal the unhappy condition of the kingdom, an undertaking rendered easier now that the great German feudal lords were succeeded by the Count of Celano and the Pope's brother Richard as Frederick's chief lieutenants. Upon this latter Frederick bestowed as a reward the fief of Sora.

Innocent was able to send some troops into Sicily for Frederick, and then returned to Rome, rejoicing in his success and with his mind freer, so that he could devote himself to the many complicated matters

which from all parts of the world came to him for
their solution. Nor was there a limit to Innocent's
activity, which regarded the universe as included in
the all-embracing nature of the Papacy, wherein his
lofty spirit found congenial expression.

We have seen Innocent as guardian of Frederick
II. and tenacious defender of his rights to the throne
of Sicily, rights which he skilfully combined with
the prerogatives claimed by the Church over the
kingdom; but, in opposition to all papal interests,
Henry VI., when dying, had left the boy already
the elected King of the Romans and heir to the
Empire. Innocent having succeeded to the Papacy
with the intention of overthrowing the whole of
Henry's work, was opposed to such a succession, and
the state of Germany was favourable to his wishes.
When Philip of Suabia, leaving Tuscany in revolt,
had hurried to Germany to maintain there the rights
of his nephew Frederick, he had found that realm
in great confusion. The Guelphs were straining
every nerve to wrest the Empire from the Hohenstaufen, and the extreme youth of Frederick II.
favoured them, as it rendered him incapable of govern-
ing so disturbed a country. Many barons refused
to recognise a child as their sovereign, and vainly
did Philip appeal to the advantages of harmony and
the rights of his nephew. The Ghibellines themselves hesitated, but fearing lest their adversaries
should prevail, they rallied round Philip in a diet
held at Mulhausen in Thuringia and offered him the
crown. At first he declined it, but seeing that a
refusal would have played into the hands of the

opposite party, he yielded to the entreaties of his followers, and on the 6th of March 1198 he was proclaimed King of the Romans.

The Guelphs did not remain inactive. After several fruitless endeavours to elect the dukes Berthold of Zahringen and Bernard of Saxony, they had recourse to Otto of Brunswick, second son of Henry the Lion and nephew of the English Richard, who loved him and had given him fiefs in his own state. His eldest brother being in Palestine, Otto might regard himself as head of the Guelph family in Europe; he had the alliance and support of the English king, was young, strong, and daring in arms, contrasting in this favourably with Philip of Suabia, less robust and warlike, but his superior in mental culture and in refinement of manners. Provided by Richard with plenty of money, he returned to Germany with a large band of followers, and on the 15th of March 1198 he was elected at Cologne. Both the elected kings tried to enter Aix-la-Chapelle to be crowned, but Otto was more fortunate, and was crowned there by the Archbishop Adolphus of Cologne, who took part with him. Philip had to content himself with receiving the crown at Mentz from the hand of the Archbishop of Tarantaise, but, to make up for this, the ceremony was graced by the jewels of the imperial treasure, which the Hohenstaufen kept in the castle of Trifels. Weighty details these in those days for deciding the validity of an election.

Civil war was now, therefore, let loose in Germany, and the two parties sought for support abroad,

Otto inclining chiefly to England, Philip to France, but both seeking the favour of the Pope. Innocent at first temporised, though from the very beginning his secret sympathies were all for Otto, nor were they so without good reason. The antagonism between the Suabians and the Church was traditional, whereas the latter had often proved the devotion of the Guelph house, which also, from having fewer interests and less history, seemed less dangerous. It was quite enough to have already one Hohenstaufen in the south and almost at the gates of Rome ; if now the imperial crown was to devolve on another, the states of the Church would again be surrounded, as they had been in the times of Henry VI. Moreover, Philip, though gentle by nature and unlike his brother, had shown himself animated by the principles of his house, and adhered to Markwald in Sicily, while the fact of his having occupied as Duke of Tuscany the lands of Matilda kept him still under the ban of excommunication. Yet, in spite of all these reasons, Innocent took his time. The two parties turned to him, each asking for papal recognition and the crown of Empire for their own candidate, Otto's partisans adding promises of unlimited devotion and of great concessions, in which the King of England joined them. On the other hand, Philip's followers were more reserved and more jealous of the imperial dignity and rights. "We have sworn to our lord," they wrote to the Pope, "to support him against every one who is disaffected or disposed to contest his supreme power and the enjoyment of his brother's possessions.

Therefore we, devoted as we are to the Holy See, implore you to grant your paternal affection to him, whom we hold most worthy of the throne. Stretch not out your hand against the rights of the Empire, and rest assured that we shall not under any pretext invade the privileges of the Apostolic See, nor allow others to invade them."

Thus, by degrees, Innocent, if not practically, at least in theory, was called on to arbitrate between the two, and this was what he wished. When Alexander III., on his election, met with Octavian, who disputed his right to the pontificate, Frederick I., invoking obsolete rights, had tried to arbitrate between them; but Alexander had repulsed him, and now Innocent placed himself between the two candidates, who did not venture to repulse him, even if they did not invoke him in so many words. The subtle papal art of founding a fixed right on every fact that occurred, on every tradition, on every temporary concession, produced much fruit during the pontificate of this jurist Innocent. There might be but a short step between this arbitration and a more complete subjection of the Empire to papal authority, and so much the more caution was required that ground might be gained rather than lost. To sound people's minds, he sent to Germany the abbot of St. Anastasius and the bishop of Sutri. This latter, exceeding his instructions, freed Philip in too great a hurry from the sentence of excommunication without waiting till certain conditions made by the Pope were fulfilled; and Innocent, to mark his disapproval of the legate's haste, deprived him of the episcopal dignity, and treated his absolution as void. Yet he only gradually declared his sympathies, and not till he saw that Otto was fairly equal to the struggle, and needed but some opportune assistance to give him every probability of winning. His aid, however, became more and more urgent, especially when the arrow of a Limousin archer had cut short the English Richard's life, and with it the chief support of the Guelph cause. Conrad of Wittelsbach, the most venerable and influential prelate of Germany, having, on the Pope's suggestion, proposed a truce which was not accepted, both candidates turned once more to the Pope, who then affirming that this question of the Empire devolved principally and finally on the Apostolic See, frankly took up the attitude of a judge examining a cause on which he is bound to pass a sentence.

About that time he made public a long document called "A deliberation on the matter of the Empire," in which he undertook to examine into the rights of the rival candidates, among which, with a fine political sense not devoid of equity, he placed first of all the boy-king of Sicily, whose election to the throne of the Romans no one thought of any longer. He carefully examined the claims of all three, ably recognising those in favour of the two Suabians, but by argumentative subtleties he destroyed them, while he strengthened those which favoured Otto. And at the end of his exposition he concluded that, for the aforesaid reasons, "We do not think it advisable to insist at present that the boy (Frederick) should obtain the Empire, and as for Philip, he must be entirely set aside for obvious reasons, and we declare that he must be prevented from usurping the Empire. We moreover propose to use our influence by means of our legate with the princes that they may either agree regarding a suitable person, or may leave it to our judgment and arbitration. For if they elect no one, after long waiting, after exhorting them to agree, after instructing them by letter, we shall make known to them our counsel, that we may not seem connivers in their discord. . . . And as this business must not suffer delay, and since Otto both in himself and by family tradition is devoted to the Church, . . . we think it will be desirable to favour him openly, to accept him as king, and when that has been arranged which should be arranged for the honour of the Church, call him to the crown of Empire."

After declaring so openly his opinion, he set himself vigorously to ensure Otto's triumph, leaving no stone unturned, trying especially to detach Philip's adherents from him and draw them over to his candidate, and this among the German barons and clergy as much as in the European courts. At the beginning of March 1201 he wrote to Otto recognising him as king, and wrote also to the principal ecclesiastics and barons of Germany reproving them for their stubbornness in continuing to disagree in spite of his admonitions, declaring that the welfare of Christendom could suffer no further delays, and that he proclaimed Otto king. His legates exerted themselves in Germany, held parliaments in which they confirmed the election of the Guelph prince, and once more included Philip and his adherents in a general sentence of excommunication. At Neuss they received the oath of Otto, who promised the Pope the maintenance and recovery of all the possessions to which the Holy See laid claim, and assistance to the Church in Sicily. He agreed to accept the advice and decision of the Pope regarding the customs of the Romans and touching the Leagues of Tuscany and Lombardy, and in the same way to be guided by the Pope in concluding peace with the King of France. On receiving the imperial crown, he was to confirm by oath and in writing all these promises.

But the attitude of the Pope, whom the Guelphs followed probably only for their interest and temporarily, displeased the Germans, justly jealous of their prerogatives regarding the royal election. Philip defended himself publicly, accusing the Pope of ambitious intrusion, and declaring that German independence would be lost if the German princes could not choose their king without the papal permission. Philip's defence was echoed by his supporters, who replied to the Pope in a direct letter, signed also by archbishops and bishops, in which this interference was repelled firmly and in strong language. Innocent then, in his turn, hastened to repel the accusations, showing that he and his legates for him had not usurped the functions and rights of the electors, but had simply exercised his own. It was not he who had elected Otto as king, nor had he pretended to the right of doing so. This right the Apostolic See had transferred to them when it transferred the Byzantine Empire to Germany and recognised it as belonging to the German princes. But they also must recognise " that the right and authority of exa-

mining the person chosen to be king, and of promoting him to the Empire, belongs to us who anoint
and consecrate and crown him. . . . What? If the
princes were to agree on electing a sacrilegious man
or a tyrant, a heretic or a pagan, are we to anoint,
consecrate, and crown such a man? Far be it from
us! And," added Innocent, "if the princes, after
being admonished and waited for, cannot or will not
agree, is the Apostolic See to remain without her
advocate and defender, and is she to suffer for their
fault?" Subtle and weighty reasons, naturally springing out of the strange grafting of the imperial interests on those of the Church, and out of their rights,
inextricably blended and constantly clashing.

CHAPTER IX.

(1201–1216.)

INNOCENT III. OTTO OF BRUNSWICK AND FREDERICK II.

THE triumph of Otto was greatly desired by Innocent, not simply for the sake of terminating this dispute in a manner favourable to the Church, but also because he felt all the benefit which would accrue to Christendom were its two great powers able to act in concord. The whole Christian world was passing then through serious changes, to some of which Innocent himself had given the impulse, while he merely seconded others. In the narrow limits of this work it is impossible to follow Innocent III. through the vast ramifications of his action, and the history of this famous Pope must necessarily remain maimed and incomplete. The character of his action was universal, and was inspired by the idea of this universality. With him the Papacy seemed for a moment to reach the position of moderator and guide of human events, and in as far as the nature of these events permitted it, Innocent really did approach that height. Sovereigns, one after another, bowed before him ; the Eastern Church for a time came nearer again to the

Western; on the Moors of Spain and the Albigenses of Languedoc were pressing mercilessly the victorious arms of two crusades, while a third was filling the thoughts of Innocent. Through his influence the voice of Fulk of Neuilly was raised to stir up the masses, pointing out to them the path leading to the Holy Sepulchre. In the meantime two still obscure men, Dominic of Guzman and Francis of Assisi, were applying to the Pope in their eagerness to guide a new democratic movement which was creeping into the Church, restless and unconscious of its strength, and not yet knowing the magnet that drew it. Science, art, and letters were sending out new and uncertain gleams, while they tormented with hopes and fears the thoughts of mankind in the new life on which it was entering. A general transformation was going on in the world.

In the hope of the imperial authority submitting and devoting itself to him, the Pope continued to favour Otto actively, while war broke out between the two rivals, and Germany was torn with dissensions. For about two years things went well with the papal favourite, and Philip of Suabia found himself deserted by many of his followers, among the rest by Herman, Landgrave of Thuringia, and Ottocar, King of Bohemia. Then Philip, reduced to extremities, turned to the Pope with magnificent offers. He would lead an army to Palestine, would give up all her territories to the Church, and make great concessions to the clergy; should his brother-in-law, Alexius Angelus, reach the throne of Constantinople, he would obtain the subjection of the Greek Church to Rome; finally, he offered his daughter in marriage to a nephew of Innocent. At the time negotiations were opened, but ended in nothing, and Innocent protested that he had only contemplated treating of Philip's return to the bosom of the Church, not of granting him the imperial crown. But after the early successes, Fortune turned her back on Otto; and the Pope's protection, though continued for some time with active energy, did not suffice to support him. The chances of war were against Otto; the principal towns surrendered to Philip either willingly or under pressure, and those same princes who had deserted him, including the Landgrave of Thuringia and the King of Bohemia, now returned to him; also the Archbishop Adolphus of Cologne was come over to his side, and on the Epiphany of 1205 repeated the ceremony of the coronation at Aix-la-Chapelle, of which Philip had become master. Otto began to be isolated, and was abandoned even by his father-in-law, the Duke of Brabant, and his brother, Henry of Brunswick. His cause seemed now lost beyond recall, and with it were endangered the interests of the Church and the plans cherished by Innocent. This latter now began to listen more favourably to the proposals repeated opportunely by Philip. He felt it was useless to continue the struggle, and perhaps also was influenced by the state of Rome, always a difficulty for the Pope, and where a party favourable to the Suabians was gradually entering even into the Curia and among the cardinals. With the mediation at first of the patriarch of Aquileia, they began to discuss some ecclesiastical business, and in a general way the peace of the Empire, for the sake of which Innocent proposed a truce between the two rivals, and sent into Germany his legates, cardinals Ugolino of Ostia, and Leo Brancaleone, who in 1207 met Philip at Spires, agreed with him regarding the principal ecclesiastical questions, freed him from all sentence of excommunication, and arranged a year's truce between him and Otto. But Innocent wanted to follow up the truce by a peace. He saw now that victory was assured to Philip, who had with him Germany, the King of France, and many European princes, while his adversary was left without any efficient support. As Frederick Barbarossa had once become aware that all his efforts were vain against Italian resistance, and had then changed his policy, so now, when Innocent recognised the strength of German resistance, he entered on a new course. Whatever happened, the Pope would remain arbitrator in the struggle for the Empire, and this was his principal object. Let us add that the German party in Sicily was now subdued, so that Philip's influence there could no longer give umbrage, while in the Countess Matilda's contested possessions and in Lombardy the imperial power was waning before municipal independence. Peace therefore with Philip offered few dangers now, and might bear good fruit, so that Innocent tried to arrive at it by persuading Otto of Brunswick that he must now resign the crown to his adversary, who offered him in compensation the hand of his eldest daughter, Beatrice, and the duchy of Suabia. But on Otto's indignant refusal, it appeared as if one more effort on Philip's part would be necessary, and he was already preparing to make it when the tragic destiny of the house of Hohenstaufen stepped in unexpectedly. Shortly before, Philip had mortally offended one of his followers, the Count Palatine Otto of Wittelsbach, a fierce and violent man, nephew to the other of the same name, who had rendered such faithful service to Frederick I. This man's anger had been aroused by Philip's refusing him his daughter's hand after having promised it to him, and after, as it appears, having hindered his contracting another alliance. He swore vengeance, and on the 21st of June 1208 at Bamberg, while Philip was reposing and talking with the Bishop of Spires and some other courtiers, Otto of Wittelsbach entered suddenly and killed him on the spot, then knocking down and wounding whoever opposed him, made his escape. Thus at the age of thirty-four closed the life of the gentlest of this Suabian house, while he was preparing to receive the imperial crown and mark a fresh page in the history of his family. By this death, if Germany was not to fall back again into all the perplexities from which she appeared to be just emerging, the darkened star of Otto of Brunswick seemed necessarily to rise again into the ascendant, while in far-off Sicily the last Suabian could scarcely as yet inspire any fear.

Innocent deplored the shocking deed, but lost no time in returning to Otto and in doing all he could to prevent other claimants from starting up and from renewing a struggle which had already pressed so hard on Church and Empire. He applied himself to the task with energy. Aware, probably, of the faults of Otto's covetous and impetuous disposition, he admonished him to moderate them while promising him his support. He addressed himself to the communes of Lombardy and the King of France to win them over to Otto; he wrote to prelates and princes in Germany exhorting them to transfer their support to him and beware of endangering the peace by another election. To conciliate the adherents of the Suabian house, he gave the necessary dispensation for the marriage of Otto with Beatrice, the young daughter of the murdered Philip, whose death was later avenged in the blood of the murderer. Otto, in a solemn assembly held at Frankfort the 11th of November 1208, was recognised without opposition, and having celebrated his espousals with Beatrice, he set out in the August of 1209 for Italy and his coronation.

In the meantime, freedom, strength, and dissensions had greatly increased in Italy, for while every day the ties binding her to Germany were loosening, the names around which German discords rallied had crossed the Alps, and the Italian factions of the Guelphs and the Ghibellines were beginning to brandish the torch of their immortal hate. Otto rapidly traversed North Italy and Tuscany without hindrance, receiving the homage of many towns and many nobles. As advocate of the Church and in her name, but without being empowered to do so, he occupied some of the Countess Matilda's lands, and in the September of 1209 entered the states of the Church at the head of a numerous army.

Innocent came to meet him at Viterbo, and perhaps some suspicions crossed his mind on seeing

Otto arrive with an armed retinue so much greater than seemed necessary, and the occupation of Matilda's lands increased the suspicion. At any rate, Otto gave a verbal promise to restore those lands, but was always able to find pretexts for not confirming the promise in writing, and Innocent, unable any longer to draw back, preceded to Rome the Emperor-elect, who followed close, and encamped at Monte Mario. Rome, meanwhile, sullenly watched the Germans, who, as usual, gave little heed to the rights she claimed, and her citizens kept a threatening guard on the left bank of the Tiber. Hardly had the ceremony of the coronation been completed in the Vatican, than Pope and Emperor separated at the bridge of St. Angelo, and Innocent returned to the Lateran. But before Otto with his men could reach the camp, the ruffled tempers of the Romans broke out into violence. In the Leonine city there was fierce fighting all day long, and Otto, after heavy loss in men and horses, had to retire at last and fortify himself at Monte Mario. Thence he sent to Innocent asking for an interview, which he was perhaps far from desiring; and the Pope, either on account of Rome's fury against the Germans or of his own suspicions, preferred treating through ambassadors. Evidently there was disagreement between them, and it appears to have arisen from the old question of Matilda's possessions.

And in truth, with regard to these possessions Otto immediately showed himself in his real colours. Throwing to the winds all the protestations and promises

made by him for so many years to Innocent, the new
Emperor, on leaving the Roman territory, turned towards Tuscia, and forcibly occupied, as forming these
possessions, all the cities of the patrimony, which he
had always solemnly declared to belong, and belong for
ever, to the Popes. Then, by flattering the principal
nobles in Northern Italy and what remained of the
German faction in the South, this Guelph placed himself all at once at the head of the Ghibellines, and
with their aid aimed in his ambition at repeating
Henry VI.'s work and carrying it to completion. The
inevitable dispute between Church and Empire was
revived by this creature of Innocent's, and bitterly did
the Pope feel the disappointment. In vain did he
reproach Otto with the oaths made to the Church. All
the more arrogant now for having humbled himself so
abjectly before, Otto answered that other oaths bound
him to maintain the dignity of the Empire and to
recover its lost rights. And he persevered in his
daring. Urged on by the factious nobility of Sicily,
he made ready to enter that realm in order to wrest
it from the Hohenstaufen. In November 1210 he
moved from Rieti to the frontier, and settled for the
winter at Capua, whose gates opened to receive him.
The excommunication pronounced against him seemed
to stimulate him to advance, and in the following
year, after becoming master of Naples and Taranto, he
was preparing, with the assistance of the Saracens and
of Pisa, to invade Sicily. Moreover, making use of the
same means as served Henry VI., he tried to blockade
Rome, so as to hinder communications with the outer
world, while within the city he found adherents in

Innocent's political and personal enemies, and drew
the prefect of Rome over to his side, making internal
difficulties for the Pope, who would thus be less able
to take measures against him. But the repentant
Innocent was now devoting that same energy to the
destruction of his work that he had formerly given
to creating it. He worked untiringly at undermining
the foundations of his enemy's power and at isolating
him. He sent serious letters to the King of France,
confessing his error, and rekindling the jealousy and
suspicion with which Philip Augustus had always regarded Otto, the relative and favourite of the English
king. He tried to place him in a bad light before
the free cities of Northern Italy, and intimated to the
bishops of those parts that they should announce the
excommunication of this Emperor, who invaded the
rights of the Church and was disposed to oppress her.
He sent the same intimation to the bishops of Germany, where he laboured still harder for Otto's destruction. Determined on a change of policy, he did
not hesitate before what he formerly had most feared,
and now regarded the old followers of the Hohenstaufen as his allies. Rather than allow Otto to hold
the Empire at the same time as he made himself master
of Sicily, it were better to try to transplant Frederick II. into Germany and turn him once more into a
German. Legate after legate was sent to Germany to
excite the leading men to desert the excommunicated
Emperor, to whom no one was bound to keep faith, as
he had not kept it to God and the Church. Let them
be on their guard against him, or he would soon reduce
them to the same condition as his kinsmen the kings of

England had reduced the English barons. He had been entirely mistaken in Otto's character, and now was the first to pay dearly for his ignorance. Let them lose no time in providing a remedy, and he would support them with all his might.

The Pope's words flew like sparks of fire through Germany, where the embers of former fires were still warm. The enemies of the Guelphs raised their heads and the Suabian party reawoke. In many of the principal sees the bishops solemnly announced the sentence of excommunication; the King of Bohemia, the Landgrave of Thuringia, the Duke of Austria again abandoned the Emperor, and the French king meantime blew upon the coals. Civil war flared up afresh with all its horrors, the Ghibellines turned to their natural head, pointed out to them by the Pope, and in the place of the fallen Otto elected Frederick II. Thus, while the Emperor was preparing to deprive the young king of his Sicilian crown, he found himself taken in flank and obliged to return. Otto, after exhorting his partisans in the kingdom to be steadfast, proceeded to Lombardy and held a diet at Lodi. Many cities, out of deference to the Pope, did not send representatives; but others were friendly, such as Bologna and Milan, this latter unchanging in her hatred of the Suabians. In March 1212, Otto IV. had returned to Germany.

Frederick II., called by Innocent to share in the great struggles now agitating and transforming Europe, entered the field of history with an eager presentiment of a memorable career. A singular man was to emerge from this stripling. His disposition, his education, the early vicissitudes of his life, the places and the age in which he lived, all contributed to make him such, and to render still more complex a character in which it may be said that the manifold elements of his nature were fused as in an alchemist's crucible. He inherited his father's false and cruel nature, but also the stronger intellect and more generous instincts of his grandfather, and from his Norman ancestors a subtle and flexible cunning, while from all there came to him greed of power and wealth, combined with a lordly prodigality. He had drunk in from the soft breezes of his native land love of art and love of pleasure, and that Italian gift of assimilating the thoughts of other countries, and of modifying them to suit his own mind. His early circumstances had taught him dissimulation and suspicion, but his lively and talented mind inclined him to a gay and cordial sociability. Growing up among experienced and cultivated men of every country, kind, faith, and profession, he had imbibed from all an inquisitive desire for knowledge, added to a mixture of superstition and scepticism in judging of life, of men, and things. He felt both hate and love strongly, and the enjoyment of taking vengeance and of conferring benefits; nor could calculation appease his passions, though it might curb them. He was highly cultivated, and of the various languages spoken in his Sicily, from the still wavering Italian to the Arab tongue, he spoke them all, and, like a knight of romance, he was a poet in more than one language, wedding the words to music. Later, he was a generous patron of science and art, a legislator, and an adept in law, and, when unbiassed by political considerations, a calm administrator of justice to his people.

To the restless spirit of the young prince a whole world was opened up by the invitation of Innocent and of the German Ghibellines, who also invoked him, and he accepted it with enthusiasm. In vain his counsellors dissuaded him; in vain his young wife, Constance of Arragon, who shortly before had given him a son, implored him to remain in his dear kingdom, far from German mists and from the uncertain glory of an undertaking fraught with danger. The proud and noble blood of the Hohenstaufen which tingled in his veins urged him on to the adventure. Having had his child Henry crowned, he intrusted the Queen with the care of the state, and in April 1212 met with a cordial reception in Rome from the citizens and from Innocent, to whose persistent protection he owed the preservation of his first crown. During his stay in Rome, Frederick made the Pope earnest declarations of unchanging gratitude and devotion, and was profuse in promises and concessions, receiving in exchange assurances of support and money to assist him in his enterprise. After separating from the Pope, Frederick proceeded by sea to Genoa, avoiding the obstacles offered to his passage by the cities and feudatories of Northern Italy, who sided with Otto, unmindful of the Pope's admonitions. Through many difficulties and dangers, accompanied by the Marquises of Este and Montferrat and a small retinue, he succeeded in getting out of Lombardy and gaining the Alps. Past Trent and the Engadine, he reached the shores of the Lake of Constance, and dashed with sixty knights into that city, which opened her gates to him only three hours before the arrival of the Emperor Otto with a larger retinue. The short delay, however, had sufficed. Constance holding out for Frederick at that moment, saved the fortunes of the Hohenstaufen and exerted a special influence over the future of the Empire.

Otto meantime had not awaited in idleness the coming of this storm, provoked by his enemies both in and out of Germany, and had devoted himself most energetically to winning over adherents among Italians and Germans, detaching as many as he could from the other side. First at Frankfurt, then at Nürnberg in diets which he summoned, he made formal complaints against Innocent, accusing him of attacking German independence and the rights of the Empire ; and while he tried to put the Pope in an unfavourable light as an enemy of the Empire, he, on the other side, did all he could to gain alliances, especially in England and Flanders, in order to have powerful forces to oppose to the persistent enmity of Philip Augustus. To attract the partisans of the house of Suabia, he decided on celebrating the marriage, already arranged, between him and the youthful Beatrice, daughter of Philip of Suabia, and heiress of his claims ; but the marriage was an inauspicious one. Four days after the ceremony the bride suddenly died, and soon dark rumours against Otto circulated concerning the unexpected event, and in those days

of party animosity the accusation, in spite of its im-
probability, did not fail to be listened to by many, and
to all this sudden death appeared an evil omen. The
Suabian and Bavarian barons held aloof from him;
and Frederick, on arriving in Germany, found the
ground well prepared, notwithstanding all his opponent's energy, and civil war flared up and spread
rapidly.

But it was not in Germany that the fate of the
Empire was this time to be determined, and Otto had a
more dangerous enemy in the powerful King of France.
An enemy to him and to his kinsmen, the English
Plantagenets, and jealous of his own powerful feudatories, especially of the Count of Flanders, who aimed
at weakening the French monarchy, just as the English
had weakened the strength of King John, Philip Augustus regarded the young Hohenstaufen as an element
of victory in the struggle which could not be deferred
much longer. On the ground therefore of their common
enemies he entered into an alliance with him, helping
him with money, as Genoa had done and the Pope,
who meanwhile was moving heaven and earth in his
favour. Frederick was making good way in spite of
manifold difficulties, but he felt how strong his adversary still was, and he clung to the Pope. In a diet at
Egra in Bohemia, whose king, Ottocar, had declared for
him, he solemnly repeated and confirmed with a golden
bull his promises to the Holy See. He maintained
and enlarged the ecclesiastical prerogatives in matters
of tenure, election, and appeal to Rome; he also promised to assure to the Church the direct possession of
her lands, including among these the territories from

Radicofani to Ceprano, all the March of Ancona, Spoleto, Matilda's possessions, Ravenna and the Pentapolis, only reserving the ancient right of forage; at the same time he recognised the suzerainty of the Pope over the kingdom of Sicily, over Sardinia and Corsica. He accompanied these concessions with words of reverential gratitude and affection. "I have before my eyes," he says to Innocent in his bull, "your immense and innumerable benefits, O my fatherly protector and benefactor, whose guardianship nourished, shielded, and promoted me since my mother Constance flung me almost from her womb into your protecting arms, and we shall always with a humble and devout heart pay our tribute of honour and obedience to our special mother the Roman Church." Singular language in the mouth of Frederick, who was to show himself later so different in word and deed!

But this language, which then was not perhaps altogether insincere, did him good service in flattering Innocent's fond but vain hope that at length there sat on the throne of the Empire a man really devoted to the Church; and in this hope Innocent continued to favour him, not only in Germany and Italy, but also with the King of France, to whom the Pope drew all the closer, as the estrangement between himself and the English king approached an open rupture. And though Innocent somewhat later made peace with England, yet his interests were always at that time with France, so that before long things came to a point at which war could not be avoided. Otto IV. united his army to the English one, and the battle of Bouvines on

the 27th of July 1214, so famous in French and
English annals, decided also the imperial destinies.
Otto, defeated, exhausted by this war, and abandoned
by his partisans, retired to his duchy of Brunswick,
henceforth in little more than name the rival of
Frederick. This latter, favoured by fortune, could
soon regard himself as the almost unquestioned lord
of Germany. On the 24th of July 1215 he made his
solemn entry into Aix-la-Chapelle, accompanied by
a great crowd of German princes, and by the French
and papal envoys. On the following day he assumed
the silver crown of Germany. As the ceremony was
completed the voice of a priest resounded through
the sacred aisles recalling that Jerusalem the blessed
was in the hands of infidels, and invoking a crusade.
Was it from an impulse of enthusiasm in that solemn
moment of his life, or was he merely yielding to a temporary political necessity ? Frederick took the Cross,
and, following his example, many princes vowed themselves with him to the crusade ; but that vow, which
seemed to bind him for ever in love to the Church, was
before long to turn into a tormenting chain, bringing
no other result but the implacable hatred of the Popes,
returned by him with equal bitterness.

Now that his candidate was firmly seated on the
imperial throne, the heresy of the Albigenses eradi-
cated, serious ecclesiastical questions disposed of in
almost every European state, and the Greek Church
united to the Roman, thanks to the new Latin Empire at Constantinople, Innocent thought it high time
to call round him the Christian fathers in a council to
be held in the Lateran. Very grand was the material

prepared for the labours of this grave assembly. To consolidate the recent conquests of the Church, to affirm in a series of canons the legislation which had gradually been developed, to expound to the world the majesty of the Papacy and the unlimited extension of all its rights and powers, but above all to reform the Church where necessary, confirm the purity of the faith, and provide for the supreme struggle between East and West which had its centre in the sepulchre of Christ—these were in Innocent's mind the principal objects of the council. On St. Martin's Day 1215 a very numerous assembly of bishops met in the Lateran, and was inaugurated by Innocent in a speech indicating the principal points they were to discuss, with a specially warm recommendation of the crusade; and among the many important decisions of the council, those concerning this sacred enterprise had great prominence. Another resolution was one recognising Frederick II. as King of the Romans, although the Milanese envoys tried to make good the claims of the forsaken Otto. On the closing of the council, Innocent gave all his attention to the crusade, which had throughout his pontificate been the distant aim of his policy, but already in his opening discourse his words mingled with a hope of new triumphs the sad presentiment of approaching death. "If it is in the designs of God," he had said, "I am willing to drink the cup of the passion, though I desire to remain in the flesh until the work begun be completed. Yet not mine, but God's will be done, and for that said I unto you, With desire I have desired to eat this passover with you before

I suffer." The presentiment was true. While going to Pisa to persuade her to join Genoa in the crusade, he was seized at Perugia by a fever, and died on the 16th of June 1216. He was but fifty-six, and for more than eighteen years he had ruled the Church among powerful princes, often at variance with him, and, what was more difficult, among nations agitated by a vague tendency to some transformation not yet understood, but giving a sense of restless discomfort. It is not for us to judge in this little book a man whose vast labours far exceeded the limits of our subject. Here we can only say that, in his relations with the Empire, he was perhaps less fortunate and less discriminating than in other matters; though even on this point a judgment is very difficult. Certainly, however, as Frederick Barbarossa had forgotten the conditions of his time, and had exaggerated the power of the Empire, so also Innocent forgot or did not see them, and exaggerated the power of the Church. Hence the grand, but, from its very nature, perishable work of both could not resist the spirit of the age.

CHAPTER X.

(1216–1227.)

HONORIUS III. AND FREDERICK II.

THE crusade which had occupied Innocent III.'s last thoughts became the chief and continual aspiration of his successor, Honorius III., who inherited besides a vast amount of business, including the papal relations with the new Emperor-elect, which soon proved perplexing. The subtle Frederick enjoyed greater freedom in his policy after the death of Innocent, whose benefits towards him had been too great to be easily ignored during his lifetime. Nor did he change his policy all at once, as his father had done, and still more harshly Otto IV., but showed himself considerate to the new Pope ; yet, while protesting his devotion to the Holy See, he began to take a new departure. During Innocent's life he had had his son Henry proclaimed King of Sicily, and at the same time he had at Strasburg solemnly promised the Pope that on assuming the imperial crown he would separate it entirely from the Sicilian one, and would surrender to his son the government of the kingdom. Upon this promised surrender of Sicily Innocent's change of policy was based, and it was of the highest importance to the Papacy. But now Frederick, without formally renouncing his promise, sent for his son Henry to Germany, thus in a way separating him from Sicily while connecting him with Germany, and preparing the way for ensuring to him that crown also. Frederick, well acquainted with the moderate disposition of Honorius and with his special aspirations, began a temporising policy, which was well imagined and for a long time successful.

Honorius continued to cherish his idea of the crusade with an enthusiasm which met with a very lukewarm response from Christendom. Vainly he called on the princes to arm for the enterprise ; every one was too much engrossed in their European affairs to have any interest to spare for this far-away holy war, and Frederick had less than any. To the entreaties of Honorius, recalling his vow and demanding its fulfilment, he opposed continual delays, giving as pretext the state of Germany and the risk of leaving it while Otto IV. might again set it in a blaze. But death soon freed him from this adversary. On the 19th of May 1218, in a castle near Goslar, Otto died, penitent and imploring humbly the Church's pardon, but not without a certain dignity ; and this death left Frederick in unquestioned possession of the Empire. Honorius invited him to Rome for the coronation, thinking thus to embark him on the road to Palestine ; but Frederick, much as he desired the crown, would not leave Germany till he had ensured the election of his son as King of the Romans. The

Curia became anxious and remonstrated, but Frederick tried by flattering the Pope's pious wishes to reassure him. According to him, the promotion of Henry had the sole object of preserving peace in Europe should he himself die in the Holy Land, and he confirmed with fresh bulls the promises given to the Church at Strasburg, and renewed his humble protests of love and duty. At the same time, he astutely asked that he might retain the kingdom of Sicily for his life-time, instead of ceding it to his son, and the Pope did not seem much disinclined to consent.

Thus time passed, and Frederick, while making many promises and talking with great zeal, continued to carry out his own purposes. But the Curia began to lose confidence in him and his promises, and gave the first hint of this by drawing near again to the Lombard Guelphs, who had always sided with Otto and regarded the Suabian with no favour. In the hope of promoting the crusade, Cardinal Ugolino of Ostia laboured energetically in restoring peace among the cities of Central and Northern Italy, and with considerable success. This harmony could never be favourable to imperial interests, but the Pope also had his difficulties at home; for the turbulent Romans had obliged him, in June 1219, to leave Rome. Still, his efforts for the deliverance of the Holy Sepulchre had about that time one successful result which appeared important: Damietta fell into the hands of the Crusaders, and with such slaughter of the infidels, writes one contemporary chronicler, that the Christians themselves regretted it. But confusion and discord among the conquerors soon reduced almost to nothing the good of the victory, and it became every day more urgent for the success of the enterprise that reinforcements should be sent and a definite expedition undertaken.

Honorius continued to insist with Frederick that he should put an end to his uncertainties and start at last, but he renewed his pretexts from month to month, till the Pope's words began to betray some bitterness of feeling, and in a letter of the 1st of October 1219 he had recourse to threats. Two other terms had been fixed for his departure, said the Pope, and, far from moving, Frederick had not even made the slightest preparation. It was time to make haste and get ready, for who could say but God reserved for him the victorious issue of an enterprise begun so long before. Let him remember his grandfather Barbarossa, who had concentrated in it all his power. Let him be mindful that unless assistance reached them soon, the Eastern Christians were in imminent risk of disaster. He allowed him one further delay till the day of St. Benedict (March 21, 1220), "but do not slumber," he admonished with mild severity, "lest, if this third term pass unheeded, thou incur excommunication." They were serious words, of which Frederick, not yet crowned Emperor, well understood the import, and Honorius reinforced them by bidding the German bishops declare all those Crusaders excommunicated who by St. Benedict's day were not ready to fulfil their vow.

So Frederick felt that it had become necessary to return to Italy, make sure of the imperial crown, and then act according to circumstances. He sent on before him the abbot of Fulda to announce his coming to the Pope, who was still at Viterbo, and to the Roman senate, whose friendship he valued all the more that he was quite determined not to give up the kingdom of Sicily. At the same time, in Germany, by making great concessions to the clergy and flattering the princes, he obtained the election of his son Henry as King of the Romans on the 1st May 1220. He did not immediately send word of this to Viterbo; but when he saw the Curia was perturbed by it, he applied himself to appeasing Honorius with protests and promises. Henry's election—so he wrote from Nüremberg in the following July—had occurred without his knowledge, although he admitted having vainly endeavoured to obtain it on former occasions. He had only agreed to it on condition that the Pope also accepted it. He quite felt that the Pope's only reason for not approving of this election was his unwillingness to see the kingdom of Sicily added to the Empire. The Church must try to banish this suspicion, for he would take care to keep them separated in every way possible, and would prove himself such a son that the Apostolic See would rejoice at having begotten him; indeed even if the Church had not already claims on the kingdom, and he were to die without heirs, he would rather leave it to the Church than to the Empire. Honorius accepted both excuses and promises, and Frederick, at the head of a brilliant army, and accompanied by his queen, Constance of Aragon, entered Italy once more.

His long stay in Germany by no means meant that Frederick desired to remain there always, or preferred it as a residence. On the contrary, he cherished the recollection of his early years spent in sunny Sicily, and had tried to settle matters in Germany so that he might again take up his abode at Palermo, and make this city the chief centre of the Empire. He was carrying out and transforming the idea of his father and grandfather, and was unconsciously following the development of the times, which were maturing a new and marvellous civilisation. For Italy was indeed rapidly unfolding her vital power, and it was so exuberant, so powerful and daring, as to fascinate Frederick's ardent and vivacious spirit. But it was not easy to make really his this Italy which pleased him so much, and whose complex and manifold life, especially north of Rome, was broken up and reflected in that of so many cities, cities encouraged by the Popes to shake off the imperial yoke, differing in traditions, interests, and politics, desirous of liberty and jealous of the lords whose tyrannies were beginning to blossom out of the democratic discords. The best he could do for the moment was to cross Italy in a conciliatory spirit, flattering the nobles in the north and encouraging their feudal interests, which in Italy were always useful to the Empire; giving as many privileges as possible to friendly cities, avoiding those whose attitude was threatening, like Milan, which he did not go near, having consequently for the present to renounce the iron crown. In this manner he came in sight of the Eternal City on the 14th of November 1220, and encamped with his army on the heights of Monte Mario.

For the first time for ages a man born in Italy

assumed in Rome the crown of the Empire, and the
Romans, who had made Otto IV. feel the weight
of their republican swords, now regarded with satisfaction the new lord of the world, who showed himself
considerate and treated them with deference. After
a cordial reception, Honorius crowned him and Constance on the 22d of November, in the midst of
peaceful demonstrations on the part of the Romans,
in the presence of many Italian and German princes
and ambassadors from various Italian towns. Also
from Sicily many barons came to do him homage, and
were gladly received by him. Frederick had succeeded
in becoming, with the Pope's consent, both King of
Sicily and Emperor. In return, he made many desired
concessions, and promulgated a series of constitutions,
which included the extirpation of heresy, unlimited
protection to the Church, and an implicit recognition of the clergy's independence from the state.
On both sides such concessions had been made as
contained in themselves the germ of discord, far
exceeding, as they did, all that Church and Empire
could possibly yield; and this germ, instead of wither-
ing, was destined to spring up stronger in consequence of Frederick's oath to proceed on the crusade
—an oath which he solemnly renewed in St. Peter's.
Ugolino, cardinal of Ostia, received his oath, and did
not forget it later, when he became Pope under the
name of Gregory IX.

Three days after the coronation Frederick left
Rome, and on the 9th of December entered his
kingdom, which had suffered during his absence
and was in great confusion. With a firm hand

he undertook to reorganise it, but his keen eye as legislator and politician recognised the impossibility of assimilating Sicily and Germany, and in creating a new code of laws for Sicily he adapted it to the people for whom it was destined, and revived in it the traditions of his maternal ancestors, from whom he inherited the beautiful realm. In this way he showed himself disposed to separate Sicily from the Empire, while in reality he was strengthening the bonds where most he wanted them to be strong. The Sicilian nobility, always factious and ambitious, had usurped a large part of the royal goods and possessions ; but he not only took back again very vigorously what had been usurped, but very much weakened the usurpers by annulling their chief prerogatives and increasing to their injury the royal authority. Among the injured nobles was Richard, Count of Sora, Innocent's brother, who had his possessions confiscated. Many barons shut themselves up in their castles and stood out, but one after another they were subdued. Some retired within the patrimony of the Church, where the Pope received them, himself discontented with Frederick for having imprisoned some bishops as inciting to rebellion. Honorius had raised loud complaints, but the Emperor was inflexible. The Saracens, meantime, had remained in Sicily, and were very troublesome by reason of their continual depredations, which made them a serious danger, so that Frederick crossed the strait determined once for all to crush them. As before in Germany, now in Italy the cares of state, so manifold, and so absorbing all his faculties and

resources, estranged him more and more from the
thought of the crusade, for which Honorius continued equally zealous, and now renewed his entreaties
and threats. Frederick found pretext after pretext
to excuse his delay, and added even further concessions, among which a decree making formal restitution of the Countess Matilda's possessions to the
Church. The Pope, however, did not seem much
impressed by a concession which the municipal life
of North and Central Italy rendered somewhat illu-
sory, and he did not cease to insist on the crusade
and reproach him for his delay. Matters were
further embittered by the news that Damietta, on
the 8th of September 1221, had fallen again into the
hands of the infidels. The echo of this misfortune
sounded sadly throughout Europe, and Honorius
blamed Frederick bitterly for it, accusing his slow-
ness and delay of being the cause of this immense
disaster.

Frederick felt it necessary to appease the Pope,
through whose words threats of anathema began to
pierce. In the spring of 1222 Pope and Emperor
had an interview at Veroli, and decided to hold in
November a general congress of princes at Verona.
There the time should be settled on for the departure
of the Christian army, which Frederick promised to
conduct in person. But this same promise contained
a delay, and he profited by it to return to Sicily to
fight with the Saracens and subdue them. During
that time the Empress Constance died, and a plan was
immediately formed for uniting the widowed Emperor
to Yolande, daughter of John of Brienne, and titular

heiress to the kingdom of Jerusalem. The Roman court encouraged an idea which might incite Frederick to the conquest of a kingdom, the right to which would come to him as his wife's dower; so the Pope received very graciously King John of Brienne, who happened just then to come to Rome. But some fresh signs of discontent among the Romans threw the aged and infirm Honorius into his old anxieties, and this and other hindrances combined with illness prevented his again meeting the Emperor till the spring of the following year 1223. This meeting no longer took place at Verona, but at Ferentino in the Campagna, and there Frederick promised on oath to start on the 24th of June 1225. Damietta having already fallen without recall, the need for assistance was less urgent, and Frederick held that two years were absolutely necessary for a peaceful settlement of his Italian possessions and to prepare ships and arms for so great an enterprise. Within two years he would marry Yolande of Brienne, to whom he then engaged himself, and his father-in-law would meanwhile go through Europe exciting all kings to join the crusade, or at least obtaining from them men and money.

For a moment it really appeared as if Frederick intended this time to keep his promise, for he began preparations for the expedition, and joined the Pope in striving to induce other sovereigns to share in it. But he also, with surprising energy and statesmanship, devoted himself to the re-settlement of the kingdom and to the encouragement of commerce and industry, founding moreover in 1224 with great magnificence a university at Naples, in which his hopes saw a future

rival to the democratic Bologna with its Guelph sympathies. Nothing vexed Frederick more than the
democracy of the Northern Italian republics, which
opposed all his ideas of absolute government with far
greater effect than did those powerful feudal lords
whom in Sicily he was putting down, and in Germany
he was obliged to tolerate. Hence he paid great
attention to Lombard affairs, determined as far as
he was able to undermine a liberty injurious to his
power, in this revealing his father's and grandfather's
instincts for imperialism. But the republics did not
belie their instincts either, and, in spite of their internal quarrels, felt that their independence was the condition of their existence. Frederick saw that to leave
them to increase in pride and prosperity while he was
engaged in distant dangers was to give up, perhaps for
ever, all hope of subduing them; yet it would probably
be difficult to bring the Pope round to further delays
which would in reality serve to destroy that Lombard
Guelphism, which the Holy See had always cherished,
even when most peacefully inclined to the Empire.

Fortune favoured Frederick. The courts of France
and England showed little enthusiasm for the crusade,
while in Rome new seditions had broken out, which had
obliged the old and enfeebled Honorius to fly, and had
recalled into the city the senator Parentius, who had
already shown himself an enemy to the clergy. In this
precarious state of things, Frederick sent to the Pope
King John of Brienne and the Patriarch of Jerusalem.
The two envoys found the fugitive Pontiff at Rieti.
They represented to him the state of things in Italy,
the indifference of other princes, the necessity of a

further delay in order to ensure success. Honorius
bowed to the force of circumstances, and yielded a last
time. It was decided, under pain of excommunication,
that in August 1227 the Emperor should absolutely
depart for the Holy Land with a hundred transports
and fifty galleys, and should there remain fighting for
two years with a thousand men-at-arms, having three
horses each; in the meantime he was to give passage
to two thousand other fighting men. In the town of
San Germano Frederick solemnly swore to these conditions in the presence of two cardinals who represented
the Pope.

But new causes of discontent soon arose between
these two powers. Honorius wished to provide for
various sees vacant in the kingdom without first con-
sulting Frederick, confining himself to asking for the
bishops' enthronement; but Frederick, jealous of the
royal prerogatives, protested, and his relations with
Rome became considerably embittered. Yolande of
Brienne arrived in Italy, and at Brindisi, the 9th of
November 1225, was married to the Emperor; but even
this contributed to his misunderstandings with Rome.
King John of Brienne, discontented at Frederick's
assuming for himself the title of King of Jerusalem
without any regard to him, began to accuse him in
Rome of unfaithfulness to his new bride, and certainly
Frederick's dissolute tendencies gave colour to the accusation. Honorius wrote to the Emperor reproaching
him with his neglect of his father-in-law's claims,
which might injure affairs in Palestine; and on John's
leaving his son-in-law's dominions, the Pope received
him with kindness, and intrusted to him the manage-

ment of some portion of the Church's patrimony. Mistrust and irritation between Rome and Sicily increased daily.

During this time, Frederick, with an eye to Lombard affairs, had convoked for the Easter of 1226 a great diet to be held at Verona, in which Italy and Germany were to be represented. But the Guelphs and Lombards were awake, and their cities, aware of the danger, began to cling more closely together, and to renew the famous league which had held out against Frederick Barbarossa. Probably more or less direct encouragement and moral support came from Rome. Certainly the announcement of Frederick's coming united every one, and promoted, at least for the time, the agreement necessary for the defence of their liberties. The Pope, requested by Frederick in the interest of the crusades, wrote to remonstrate with the Lombards, who attended but little to him, perhaps not believing him to be in earnest. All this strengthened Frederick's suspicions of the Curia, and in March 1226, collecting an army at Pescara, he marched into the duchy of Spoleto, under the pretext of levying troops who should accompany him into Lombardy. The inhabitants refused, unless they had orders from the Pope, whose subjects they claimed to be ; and over this Honorius and Frederick wrangled while the Lombards collected their forces and ratified the League. From Spoleto Frederick, avoiding Faenza and Bologna, which were absolutely hostile, moved on towards Cremona, but slowly, in order to give his son Henry time to reach him there from Germany with the strength of the army ; and Henry did get as far as Trent, but could not pass the locks of the Adige, guarded by the Veronese, so that after some useless waiting he had to return. Frederick held the diet at Cremona, but it was attended by few Lombard cities. From the small number of his supporters present he could calculate how numerous his absent enemies were, and recognise the need of prudence; so, after placing the cities of the League under the ban of the Empire, he retired to Apulia, and had recourse to the Pope as mediator between him and the Lombards.

He did not hope much from the mediation, but it gave him an opportunity for gaining time, and might draw the Pope over to his own interests and create reasons for fresh delay. Meanwhile, to regain the Pope's good-will, he sent into Asia four hundred men-at-arms, and also yielded in the question of the bishops, admitting them to their sees without further opposition. The Lombard cities, on their side, were not opposed to papal mediation, from which they looked for favour; so they sent their representatives to Rome, while the Emperor's plenipotentiaries were the arch-bishops of Reggio in Calabria and of Tyre, with the Grand Master of the Teutonic Order. Honorius, being very anxious to obtain the peace necessary for the interests of the crusade, pronounced on the 5th of January 1227 the sentence of arbitration. The Emperor was to give free pardon to all Lombard cities and nobles who had joined the League; he annulled every sentence against them, and especially that which abolished the Studio of Bologna, that, however, had remained without effect; the prisoners taken on both sides were to be returned; the Guelph cities were to make peace with the Ghibellines, and to furnish to the Emperor for two years, at their own expense, four hundred men-at-arms for the crusade. The imperial decrees against heretics were put in vigour, and every act contrary to ecclesiastical liberty was revoked. The Emperor, who was at that moment powerless for opposition, agreed to everything, but with the firm intention of breaking the peace as soon as possible. The Lombard cities also approved, though without dissolving the League or loosening the ties which gave them strength. The pious Honorius flattered himself that he had secured peace. Encouraged by this hope, he sent his legates throughout Europe to rouse up every one to that sacred undertaking, which had been the aspiration of his ten years' pontificate, but his efforts were suddenly interrupted by death on the 18th of March 1227.

CHAPTER XI.

(1227–1230.)

GREGORY IX. AND THE CRUSADE — FIRST CON-TENTIONS WITH FREDERICK II. UP TO THE PEACE OF SAN GERMANO.

THE pontificate of Honorius had, on the whole, been favourable to the Emperor; and the gentle disposition of that Pope, in spite of many grounds of complaint, had never belied the good-will which as cardinal he had shown the youthful Frederick. Ugolino, cardinal of Ostia, who succeeded him under the name of Gregory IX., was of a temper little disposed to tolerance, and was resolved to conquer the Emperor's reluctance regarding the Holy Land, towards which his thoughts persistently turned. Nephew of Innocent III., he owed to him his first promotion, had earned great weight in the councils of Honorius, and was made use of by him in many difficult missions, especially in Germany and Italy, for the cause of the Cross. Matthew Paris depicts him as extremely aged, but facts do not appear to bear out his assertion, which has been recently questioned, and certainly the determined vigour of his pontificate betrays no sign of senility. He was a

man of lively faith, of great ardour; he was experienced in business, and had in his long and frequent journeys come in contact with the principal men
in Italy and Germany. In his youth he had, like
his uncle Innocent, imbibed much of his learning
at Paris and Bologna, and had had for his master
in jurisprudence the celebrated Gratianus, whose
famous collection he was later, when Pope, to incor-
porate in those decretals which still bear the name
of Gregory IX. With a quick perception of possible
advantage to the Church, he had drawn near to St.
Dominic and St. Francis, had encouraged them in
founding their famous orders, and had helped in the
diffusion of them, as if foreseeing all the services
which they would render him later in Europe and
the East.

He was on good terms with Frederick, with whom
he had had frequent dealings when cardinal. On
his election, Frederick wrote to congratulate him,
and he began by showing himself very friendly, and
urged the Lombards to be punctual in fulfilling the
conditions determined on by the arbitration of his
predecessor. But the friendliness was not unmixed
with suspicion, and in his very first letters he reminded Frederick of the engagement he had entered
into in taking the cross, and of the absolute necessity of his keeping it unless he meant to force the
Church to break with him, putting himself thereby into difficulties from which the Pope, however
anxious to do so, would be unable to extricate him.
He also sent him a brother of the new order of the
preachers to stir him up and persuade him to come

to a decision, and at the same time he was writing to the kings of France and England, and to all the bishops of Christendom, insisting on the long-delayed crusade. Frederick's position had become serious. He was bound by his repeated oaths as in the coils of a serpent. He could not shake them off, and had freely accepted the condition of excommunication if, by the approaching August, he had not set sail for the East. Nor at that moment could he find pretexts for delay, as German affairs were tolerably quiet, and it was not possible to break off suddenly the peace just agreed to with the Lombards, however much he disliked it. There was nothing for it but to yield. So that while at Gregory's request he was supplying with Sicilian corn Rome, then suffering from dearth of provisions, his son King Henry was holding a diet in Germany to invite the German crusaders to collect at Brindisi, and after many other preparations Frederick was able in the June of 1227 to announce to the Pope that his departure was at hand.

Gregory was rejoiced beyond measure, and did all he could to promote a numerous concourse at Brindisi of crusaders from all directions, and the Germans responded eagerly to the call under the leadership of Lewis, Landgrave of Thuringia, and the Bishop of Augsburg. But the crowding together in a small space, the scarcity of provisions, the stifling and unhealthy climate, told upon the troops, who suffered from a raging mortality, and as a consequence there arose a panic among the survivors, who began to waver and disperse. Frederick on arriving at Brindisi from Sicily, and seeing the dismay continually increase, hastened to embark the troops. He himself sailed from Brindisi on the 8th of September 1227, and it appeared as if at length his vow was to be fulfilled. But hardly had the anchor been weighed when sickness broke out among the soldiers, not sparing the leaders, the Land-grave of Thuringia and the Bishop of Augsburg being smitten by it. Frederick himself was seized with fever, and under the impression that he could not bear the voyage, he returned three days after he embarked and landed at Otranto, while the greater part of his men pursued their journey.

When the news reached Gregory at Anagni, great was his wrath and sorrow, and he did not restrain his feelings. He saw the destruction of all his dearest hopes at the very moment when they seemed fulfilled, and the disappointment revived his invincible mistrust of Frederick; nay, more, gave him the certainty that he was deceiving the Church and had betrayed her in every act. Frederick vainly tried to excuse himself, alleging the unexpected illness which forced him to return; the Pope would not believe him. On St. Michael's day in the chief church of Anagni, sur-rounded by cardinals and a large number of clergy, Gregory declared Frederick to have fallen under that very sentence which he himself at San Germano had invoked upon his own head, and solemnly laid him under the ban of the Church.

This terrible decision was announced to bishops and princes in a letter admirable for its precision and force of language. In it Gregory reviewed the whole of Frederick's history, from the day when he of his own

accord took the vow at Aix-la-Chapelle, without any pressure, or even knowledge on the part of the Church. He
had renewed his vow on assuming the imperial crown,
and on several other occasions, invoking excommunication upon himself if he failed to fulfil his engagement ;
and now, continued Gregory, see how he has kept
his word ! Vainly admonished by Honorius III. and
himself, he had prepared nothing for the armed masses
who were to congregate at Brindisi for the expedition,
and when they, trusting in his promises, had presented
themselves at the tryst, they found themselves without
every necessary of life, in the hottest part of summer,
in a deadly and fever-stricken air, and had died in
multitudes, plebeians and nobles alike. Then, when
they had at last sailed, he had deserted them in the
most cowardly manner, returning to the delights of his
realm and making frivolous excuses of illness. Thus
the Church had been betrayed by the son whom she
had cherished, and from whom she had already, for
the sake of this holy enterprise, endured patiently and
in silence many offences and serious injuries. This
grieved her much, but still greater was her sorrow for
the Christian army destroyed, not by the swords of
the enemy, but by these calamities, and for the remnant abandoned without a leader to the stormy sea,
and drifting no one knew whither, with little profit to
the Holy Sepulchre, and without its being even in his
(the Pope's) power to console and succour them.

Gregory ended by announcing the excommunication of the Emperor, expressing at the same time
a hope that he would repent and amend the error of
his ways. Frederick then sent envoys to justify his

conduct to the Pope, who had returned to Rome. But Gregory stood firm though he did answer him, reminding him once more of the many grounds for discontent, and, with all the diplomatic skill of Rome, grafting on to the lamentations regarding the Holy Land new complaints of many of Frederick's acts relating to the Sicilian kingdom. So things grew more and more complicated, and an understanding between them became more difficult. Frederick, finding every effort to appease the Pope was vain, took up the same complaining tone in self-defence, addressing himself to the European princes, and bitterly accusing the unrestrained ambition of the Popes, which intruded itself everywhere, and had such a thirst for universal power as left no crown secure of its authority. Now the Pope was turning against the head of the Empire. It was perfectly false that he had interrupted his voyage for frivolous motives. He appealed to God. The Curia had become a den of ravening wolves; its legates greedy of gold, contemptible, puffed up with vain knowledge, desirous of power; whereas once on a time the primitive Church, peopled by saints, had shone through its simplicity and contempt of all worldly greatness. The walls of the sacred temple were perhaps about to crumble on their insufficient foundations; let the princes meantime be ready to oppose such avarice and iniquity.

With these letters a new era of struggle was opening out between the Empire and the Papacy, and in Frederick's words we catch glimpses of a new feeling, indicating a change in the way of regarding the Church and in the manner of opposing her. We need not see in them, as others have seen, a real presage of the Reformation, but rather—unconscious, perhaps, and instinctive—that spirit of critical and disparaging research which caused heresy at that time to be springing up everywhere close to the seraphic ardours of the friar of Assisi and the austere visions of St. Dominic. And here, on the threshold of this new contest, it is well to note the fact. Frederick was never moved by that mystic and reforming spirit which, in different ways and with different motives, stirred before him Arnold of Brescia, and later Martin Luther and Savonarola. By secret paths, unknown to him and little known to us, his thought attached itself to antiquity and to the East, and Dante knew well what he was saying when he placed him, among other great men of his time, down in the uncovered graves where his powerful imagination placed the followers of Epicurus—" Che l'anima col corpo morta fanno."

Having come to this rupture with the Pope, Frederick tried in every way to create hindrances for him, so as to make him less formidable ; and he began to flatter the Roman nobles, and especially drew over the Frangipani by gifts and concessions. In the city there had already crept in some discontent with Gregory, whose authority was rather burdensome, and of this the imperial party took advantage to raise troubles. On the 27th of March 1228, the Pope, at the celebration of mass at St. Peter's, began a violent sermon against Frederick ; but he was interrupted furiously by the Ghibellines, and torn amidst insults from the altar. He had to fly, and wandered among

the cities of Sabina and Umbria, till he took refuge
at Perugia, where he remained about two years, but
did not spend his exile in idleness. He, too, profited
by the old rebels of Sicily, trying to instigate them to
new revolts and new conspiracies against Frederick.
Thus Pope and Emperor, holding all means fair in war,
lowered themselves to plotting intrigues against each
other in the dark.

But Frederick II. was not a man to lose himself in
these small squabbles, and while using them as means
to his end, he kept clearly in view the high policy of
the Empire, which was at war with a policy not less
wide in its scope. For him to have remained now in
Europe under the imputation of having deserted his
soldiers would have been both ignominious and a triumph to the Papacy and the Guelph party, which was
already too powerful in Lombardy. It was best by a
brilliant stroke to disprove the accusation, to force the
Pope to silence, and to conciliate him anew after having
diminished his authority and prestige. He began by
insisting that he had really wished to go to the
crusade, and that he still intended to do so, and his
declarations, sent about everywhere, were read also
publicly in Rome on the Capitol by the consent of the
senate, who favoured him. Under pressure from the
Pope, many bishops of the kingdom had published the
bull of excommunication, and the churches were coming under the interdict when Frederick gave the most
stringent orders that the sanctuaries should be all
opened, and by threats of confiscation he obtained
obedience from the clergy, who perhaps regarded the
papal severity as excessive. Then, having sent five

hundred more knights to the East under his marshal, Richard, he convoked a great parliament of the barons of the realm at Bari, as many and various difficulties had hindered another and larger meeting which he had previously called at Ravenna. In this meeting he arranged everything for shortly betaking himself to the Holy Land, and this sort of testament was of greater importance, because not long before the Empress Yolande had died at the birth of a son, whom he had called Conrad, so that in case of his own death there was no dearth of heirs to the kingdom. His subjects were to live during his absence in peace under the laws prevailing in the time of the good King William, and under the regency of Rainald, Duke of Spoleto. Were the Emperor to die, he named as his successor in the Empire and the kingdom his first-born, Henry, and should Henry die without heirs, the lately-born son Conrad. An oath to observe these and other dispositions was taken by the Duke of Spoleto, called to the regency, the Grand Justiciary Henry of Morra, and other barons; then some time after, Frederick, embarking at Brindisi, started for Palestine, this time in real earnest.

Gregory IX. saw in his departure only contempt for papal authority and anathemas, and his wrath increased. Forgetting that concord was indispensable for the success of the expedition, he, instead of proposing terms for the absolution of the infidel crusader, hurled maledictions after him, and openly exerted himself to raise difficulties for him in the East and to oppose him in the kingdom of Sicily—an unpardonable error, equally fatal to the crusade

and to Italy. Frederick arrived in Asia, preceded
by a great reputation and esteemed by the Saracens
as powerful, wise, and magnanimous above all the
other monarchs of the Empire, while among their
own princes there was much discord, of which advantage might have been taken both in the operations
of war and in the negotiations for peace. He was at
first received with joy at Ptolemais, where he had
landed in the September of 1228, and all expected
the papal absolution to arrive soon after him ; instead
of which, two Franciscans came from Perugia bearing the confirmation of the sentence, and forbidding
all to share in his counsels or his undertakings. A
sudden chill fell upon every one. The Patriarch, the
clergy, the Knights Templars, and many Lombard
and English crusaders fell off from him ; the Venetians hesitated ; the only ones to remain faithful were
the Pisans and Genoese, his own German and Sicilian
soldiers, and the Teutonic knights.

In spite of this, Frederick moved forward resolutely towards Jerusalem with as many as would
accompany him, while the others followed him at
a distance as if under a spell, unwilling to desert
him, and not daring to join him in the face of the
papal prohibition. When threatened along their
route by the Sultan of Damascus, it became necessary to unite, that their division, in the presence of
the enemy, might not lead to a disaster. Frederick
tried in every way to gain over his rebellious followers, but they met him with sullen resistance, and
he was forced to have recourse to an expedient very
bitter to his pride,—furling the imperial standard,

and taking the vague title of head of the Christian republic. Thus reunited and in at least apparent harmony, the crusaders resumed their suspended march, and on the 15th of November 1228 arrived at Joppa, where they fortified themselves. But even when united the Christian forces were scanty in comparison with those of the Moslems, among whose princes, however, discord reigned, though unfortunately they were not ignorant of the mis-understanding between the Pope and the Emperor. This latter received, meanwhile, melancholy tidings from his kingdom, where his return was invoked. His position was one of danger; the Pope with his anathemas was weakening him, and he was sur-rounded by lukewarm friends and underhand enemies; while, were the Saracens for a moment to forget their private animosities, all might be lost for ever. Profiting by the admiration of these Orientals, whom he himself, free from any Christian fanaticism, warmly admired, he had from the beginning entered into communication with them, in order, if possible, to reach by means of treaty the object which seemed un-attainable by force of arms. These negotiations, after being interrupted, were resumed, and peace was con-cluded with the Sultan of Egypt, who showed a more pliant disposition from the fear that Frederick would assist a nephew of his who was threatening rebellion. In the capitulation agreed to, besides a truce of ten years and the liberation of all prisoners, the Sultan gave up the towns of Jerusalem, Bethlehem, Nazareth, Said, and many other cities and castles, only reserv-ing for himself the custody of the temple at Jerusa-

lem and the privilege for the Saracens to worship in
it as freely as the Christians. The sceptical and
excommunicated Emperor had reached a goal before
which the forces of the most powerful European monarchs had long been repulsed, and the religious
ardour of infinite multitudes had exhausted themselves
in vain.

Strangely enough, success reached by this channel
increased the Pope's irritation, as he thought the
Church was entirely excluded from all merit in the
deliverance of the Holy Sepulchre—a deliverance, too,
but partial, as the infidels could still cross its threshold
and defile it with their impure prayers. Even the
Eastern clergy were ill satisfied with the results, impo-
tent though they had been to obtain better ones; and
without having in any way assisted Frederick, now
they accused him of not having done enough, and
seconded the Pope in his merciless system of persecution. Frederick behaved with moderation. He felt
he had obtained all that was possible, and had freed
himself before the world from the vow which had
weighed upon him so heavily for so many years. On
the 17th of March 1229 he entered the Holy City
with great pomp, but no prelate had courage the next
day to celebrate mass before him or to crown him.
The papal ban was suspended over his head, but
Frederick, with prudent dignity, did not meet it with
violence. Entering the crowded temple, he stepped to
the altar, stripped of its sacred ornaments, and, taking
the crown, placed it himself on his own head without
any priestly benediction. The army was irritated
with the Church, and its indignation found an echo

in Germany and Italy, where it was murmured that
the Pope had been the ruin of a glorious enterprise.
As a contemporary chronicler on the imperial side
says: "It seems probable that had the Emperor gone
in the peace and grace of the Roman Church, the
expedition to the Holy Land would have prospered far
better." On returning from Jerusalem to Ptolemais,
Frederick found a still worse reception, and much
sedition fomented by the minor friars and the Dominicans, who went on preaching against him, and whom
he in his bitterness ordered to be flogged. His chief
enemy was the patriarch of Jerusalem, who fomented
the Pope's wrath and instigated the fresh anathema
pronounced against him for having concluded an
execrable peace. Frederick, anxious to return to his
kingdom, and to combat his great adversary on closer
terms, finally left Asia at the beginning of May 1229,
and on the 10th of June was again in Apulia. He
left behind him an unfavourable impression among
the Christians, but a greatly increased reputation
among the infidels, to whom he had often shown such
kindness as enabled his opponents to accuse him of
impiety.

The affairs of the kingdom, and indeed of the whole
peninsula, were in great confusion. In Northern Italy
the Guelphs, encouraged by the repeated excommunication of the Emperor, had increased in daring against
the Ghibellines, and the country was inflamed by factions. In the kingdom, Rainald, titular Duke of Spoleto, as the Emperor's vicar during his absence, had
begun by putting down certain nobles encouraged by
Rome to rebel. John of Brienne, the now hostile

father-in-law of the Emperor and leader of the papal troops, threateningly approached the frontier, till Rainald, taking the offensive, passed it and entered the duchy of Spoleto and the March of Ancona with his soldiers, including the Saracens of Lucera, who, pushing on, did havoc to as many priests as they could lay hands on.   Gregory IX., having excommunicated Rainald, raised a great army, called in the Guelphs of Lombardy and Central Italy to assist, and poured all these forces into the kingdom in order to force Rainald to leave the Marche.   Thus the seat of war was again removed thither, and that fair and unhappy realm was devastated with fire and pillage by bands of men calling themselves "Clavesignati," from the keys of St. Peter, which they wore on their breast.   In spite of the imperialists' efforts, they made great progress, advancing into the interior, taking possession of many towns, and throwing the whole country into disorder.

Things were in this troubled state when Frederick landed at Brindisi, and his presence alone sufficed to change the whole aspect of affairs.   The "Clavesignati" drew back and recrossed the Volturno, while Frederick, uniting the returning crusaders to such troops as had remained faithful to him in the kingdom, quickly collected a good army.   But before proceeding against the pontifical soldiers he tried once more to prevail on the Pope to accept peace, and for this purpose sent to him the Archbishop of Reggio and Bari, the Grand Master of the Teutonic Knights, and the Count of Malta. Gregory only replied by a repetition of his interdicts, and Frederick moved on his troops.   The war, conducted with great vigour, was favourable to him and the soldiers of the Church were very soon disbanded, and almost all driven back beyond the Garigliano. It was in vain that Gregory, undismayed by the defeat of his champions, heaped up anathemas, proclaimed the Emperor's downfall, and had recourse to the bishops of Europe for men and money. The fortune of war continued to smile on Frederick, and Gregory soon felt it necessary to incline towards peace.

And peace indeed was also desired by the Emperor, for on account of this quarrel with the Pope, his well-considered expedition to Palestine, instead of benefiting him, was brought up against him as a crime. He also recognised the indifferent attitude of the European princes, while there could be no doubt of the threatening signs which darkened the horizon in North Italy and Germany. He therefore called before him to Capua some German princes and bishops, who, after receiving his instructions, went to see the Pope, and they had from him a kindly welcome, first at Perugia and afterwards in Rome; for about that time the Romans, alarmed by inundations and disease, recalled the Pontiff, whom nearly three years previously they had threatened and driven into exile.

The negotiations lingered on, beset with difficulties, but at last, in July 1230, they came to a satisfactory conclusion, leaving open only one question regarding the cities of Gaeta and Sant' Agata, which Frederick wanted back and the Pope was disinclined to yield. The matter was left to arbitration, and was to be decided within a year. As for the rest, Frederick pardoned all those who had fought against him, made restitution to the Church of all her territories, and of

all their possessions to the convents, recalled to their
sees all the bishops he had excluded, promised the
clergy exemption from collects and impositions, freedom of election, and independence from secular judges.
Prelates, barons, and communes chosen by the Pope
guaranteed the fulfilment of these obligations, sworn to
by the Emperor, who finally received absolution at San
Germano in the Pope's name. Thus, while forced by
Frederick's victorious arms to yield, the Pope, thanks
to his own obstinate firmness, the precarious condition
of Italy and Germany, and to his still great authority
in Europe, was able to obtain very advantageous conditions from Frederick, without in reality giving up
anything himself, except lamentations about what it
was no longer any good claiming. In the following
September both Pope and Emperor had a long interview at Anagni and separated on amicable terms, one
returning to Rome, the other to his kingdom. Peace
again settled down between Papacy and Empire, but
it was a gleam of sunshine, destined to be only too
soon overclouded.

CHAPTER XII.

(1230-1241.)

FREDERICK II.'S STRUGGLES WITH THE LOM-
BARDS—THE POPE FAVOURS THE LOMBARDS
—FREDERICK II. IS AGAIN EXCOMMUNICATED
—DEATH OF GREGORY IX.

PROFITING by the leisure which he enjoyed after this
reconciliation, Frederick II. turned his attention to
re-ordering the laws of the kingdom and putting them
in harmony with the times, which seemed throughout
Europe to call for reforms in legislation. Assisted
by jurists educated in the traditions and in the school
of Roman law, Frederick's work showed in many
ways a distinct progress, and opened the path to the
modern development of public and private law. Re-
suming the work of his Norman predecessors, which
had suffered from time and from long disturbances
in the kingdom, Frederick modified it, in great part
trying to restrict feudal rights and to oppose to
them a strong monarchy, sure of itself and more
careful of the general interests of the people than
of the privileges of the nobility and higher clergy.
It was a wise and provident measure, but it excited
opposition in many nobles, because detrimental to

their prerogatives, while Rome was offended at the clergy's privileges being curtailed, and at the increase of strength in a monarchy which she regarded with suspicion, and over which she laid claim to suzerainty. Nor could the severe laws introduced then by Frederick against heretics counterbalance this unfavourable impression, for they merely corresponded to the spirit of the times, and were, after all, no severer than those in force elsewhere. Heresy, which was springing up everywhere, was in the eyes of legislators a state crime and to be quenched in blood, so that Frederick in this respect made no concession to the Church, and merely recognised in his laws an idea then universal, and which appeared to no one either harsh or unjust.

While doing all he could by legislation to strengthen his authority in the kingdom, Frederick did not lose sight of the Lombard republics, who, on their side, were watching him with suspicion. They foresaw danger to themselves in the peace concluded between him and the Pope at San Germano, and also in these same laws, promulgated by him too distinctly in support of the royal prerogatives not to give umbrage to those staunch republicans as much as to the Sicilian barons. Wherefore, ceasing from their constant civil warfare, several Lombard cities began to league themselves together against the common enemy. Meantime, Frederick had convoked for All Saints' day 1231 a diet at Ravenna, to which all the cities and feudatories of North Italy were invited, and his son Henry was to come from Germany. The Pope promised to prevail on the

Lombards to attend the diet, and he did send for the purpose the bishops of Brescia and Vercelli to the Guelph towns; but either the bishops were lukewarm in their exhortations or the towns were too determined in their opposition; certainly the Pope's good offices produced no effect, and the leagued cities resolved at Bologna in October to collect an army and prepare for war. The Pope's conduct did not satisfy Frederick when he found at Ravenna only a few feudatories and the envoys from some Ghibelline towns, nor were his suspicions perhaps wholly groundless. On one side and the other the scarcely suppressed antagonism broke out afresh, for it had its roots in the very essence of things. It was impossible for Frederick not to strain every nerve to secure his unquestioned authority in Lombardy; equally impossible was it for the Pope to give him hearty assistance in beating down those Guelph communes to which he could look for support in every quarrel with the Empire. Thus on both sides there was formed a gradual accumulation of reasons for latent mistrust, which only needed a spark to make it flare up at any moment.

King Henry had not been able to take part in the Diet of Ravenna from the Lombards having closed the passage of the Alps against him towards Verona with a powerful body of troops, and thus hindered his entering Italy. This fact grieved Frederick the more that his authority suffered much from it, not in Italy only, but also in Germany, where some threatening signs of rebellion gained more serious import from a fear that his own son encouraged them, and was disposed, as king in Germany, to throw off all allegiance to his father. Hence Frederick placed under the ban of the Empire those Guelph cities which had not sent envoys to Ravenna; and though mistrusting the Pope, he tried to keep on good terms with him, so as to be able safely to leave Italy and settle the German affairs in person. He therefore left Ravenna for Aquileia, where he met his son, who, affirming his fidelity on oath, tried to banish all suspicion from his mind, and apparently for the moment succeeded. The Emperor returned from Aquileia to Apulia, where he found new troubles. The tendency in his reign to enforce the absolute authority of the sovereign did not displease the nobles and clergy only, but stood in the way of the municipalities, jealous of their old prerogatives and desirous to acquire new ones. A revolt broke out in Sicily which was stifled in blood, and it appears that on that occasion many political offenders were simply burnt as heretics, and the laws intended for religious persecutions served the astute Emperor as instruments of human vengeance. Later, the Pope reproached him with this fact, and used it as an accusation against him.

However, both parties had to feign a desire for peace, which neither felt. Hence, after further negotiations, it was resolved to ask the Pope a second time to arbitrate between Frederick and the Lombards. In the winter of 1232 the delegates from the republics, and for the Emperor the archbishop of Messina, the bishop of Troia, the grand justiciary Henry of Morra, and the famous Pier della Vigna, all met at the papal court to discuss their reciprocal claims and

rights. The Pope pronounced his decision on the 5th of
June 1233. In it he left everything much as it was
after the arbitration of 1227, showing great partiality
towards the Lombards. That necessity of things of
which we have already spoken led him to this verdict,
and, indeed, so also did justice towards the now well-
established rights of Lombard liberty. Frederick
naturally resented the sentence bitterly, even complained of it, but did not refuse to accept it, and for
the moment tried to dissimulate his feelings. Serious
difficulties drew Emperor and Pope together, and the
need they had of each other made them use caution
and forbearance in their mutual relations. As if to
compensate Frederick for this unfavourable sentence,
the Pope sent into Lombardy his legates and mission-
aries to preach peace, and among them one John of
Vicenza, a Dominican, who for some time aroused
great enthusiasm among the masses in various towns,
then lost credit and disappeared. In reality, rather
than peace there prevailed on every side a warlike
feeling, encouraged not only by the difference of interest between the communes and the Empire, but also
by the factious party spirit in the towns and by the
private ambition of many noblemen, who hoped by the
help either of Guelphs or Ghibellines to rise in the
state. The guiding spirit of the Ghibelline faction
and the Emperor's right hand in Lombardy was
Eccelin da Romano, whose family found a powerful
rival in that of the Guelph Este.

Nor was it only in Lombardy that party spirit ran
high, but throughout Tuscany and in Rome herself it
lifted its head against the Pontiff, and after many

alternations of turmoil and quiet, at last forced him to
fly from the city and take refuge in Rieti. Thence
Gregory IX. hurled anathemas against the Roman
senate, wrote from all parts asking for help in soldiers
and money to subdue the rebels, and invoked Frederick's assistance. The Emperor thought the occasion
a good one for gaining over the Pope, detaching him
from the Lombard Guelphs and obtaining his influence
to thwart the now open intrigues going on against him
in Germany at his son's court. In May 1234 Frederick, going to see the Pope at Rieti, presented to him
his other son, Conrad, in whom his best hopes were
now centred, and then laid siege to the castle of Ris-
pampano, obstinately defended by the Romans. Owing
either to their gallant resistance or to Frederick's in-
tentionally lukewarm attack, the siege lasted fruitlessly
for two months, and in September, Frederick, alleging
the impossibility of taking the fortress, left it and returned to Apulia, of which the Pope complained loudly,
accusing Frederick of bad faith and of a secret understanding with the Romans. Nor did it avail anything
that Frederick had left behind him a strong body of
German soldiery, who joining the men of Viterbo, then
threatened by Rome, inflicted a serious defeat on the
Romans, and having entered Sabina, brought again
that territory under obedience to the Pope. In spite
of this, Gregory's complaints continued, but no open
rupture followed. The relations between the two in
those days, in their mixture of friendliness and hostility,
exactly represent their ever-recurring suspicions and
necessities, which drew them together and separated
them at one and the same time.

Meanwhile Gregory IX. after having canonised St. Dominic at Rieti in July 1234, had returned to Perugia, whence he repeatedly invoked the assistance of Christendom in favour of the Holy Land, where things were rapidly growing worse. Frederick had responded favourably to the Pope's exhortations, when new events obliged him to turn all his care and attention to the North. His son Henry was conspiring against him in Germany, and allying himself to the Guelph cities of Lombardy, being enticed into doing so by Milan, who dangled before his eyes the iron crown of Italy, which had not been granted to his father. This offence sunk deep into Frederick's heart, and the cruel instincts of his vindictive nature were aroused by the disloyalty of his son in joining his most deadly foes. The Pope saw that this conspiracy would compromise the expedition to Palestine, and therefore seconded the Emperor's going to Germany about Easter 1235. His presence there was quite enough to restrain every thought of rebellion, so that Henry, abandoned by all, had no alternative but to throw himself at his father's feet and implore his pardon, and Frederick was more clement than the offence would have led one to expect. However, the ill-advised prince was deprived of every dignity, and was kept as a prisoner in several fortresses, first in Germany, then in Apulia, where he died some years later. Frederick showed great grief at his death, and the grief was perhaps unfeigned, for his ardent and impressionable nature could easily contain mixed feelings of love and hate.

A few days after Henry's submission the Princess Isabella, sister of Henry III. of England, arrived in

Germany, and her nuptials with the Emperor were solemnised at Worms. The Pope was much pleased at this marriage, which he had for some time been trying to bring about, in the hope of its serving to separate the Suabian interests from those of the house of France, and of its supplying him in any case with a weapon, offensive and defensive, against the Empire. But although these various events in Germany seemed calculated to bring Frederick and the Pope nearer together, in Italy things were different, as the Pope could not succeed in reconciling the Lombards with the Emperor, and a war seemed imminent, in which the Church and the Empire were unlikely to find themselves in accord. Determined at any rate to break the strength of the Lombard league, Frederick reached Verona in August 1236 at the head of a numerous army, and all the Ghibellines of Lombardy rallied round him.

Fighting began, and all that year there were constant engagements, mostly to the Emperor's advantage, but to the great injury of the country. It is true the Pope continued to exhort every one to peace, but in reality his relations with Frederick became more and more strained. On both sides there was a perpetual bandying of complaints, of imputing to each other bad faith and usurpations. The Pope was exceedingly vexed with Frederick for attending to Lombardy instead of to Palestine, he mourned over the infringement of ecclesiastical rights in Apulia and Sicily, over the prosperous Saracenic colony at Lucera, and hinted that the Romans were secretly led on by him to rebel, while the Emperor haughtily justified himself, and denied the truth of the Papal

assertions.   Italy was his, he said, and till he had
reduced it to submission he had no mind to risk losing
it by setting off for Palestine.   He did not intend to
yield a jot of his rights, and Gregory, by helping the
enemies of the Empire, was trying to usurp them without reason and without conscience.   And indeed Frederick had grounds for suspecting the Pope's envoys
sent into Lombardy to treat of peace, and held them
to be encouraging the League rather than to be messengers of peace and anxious for the maintenance of imperial rights.   At any rate, Frederick was determined
to subdue the Lombards, who, mindful of the past,
resisted as their forefathers had resisted Barbarossa.
During all the year 1236 and a great part of 1237
the war continued, but without coming to a decisive
engagement.   Finally, the two parties attacked each
other near the banks of the Oglio at Cortenuova, and
there the Lombards suffered a terrible defeat, leaving
on the field many thousands among dead and prisoners,
while the *Carroccio* of the Milanese remained as a
trophy of victory in the hands of Frederick, who re-
entered Cremona in triumph.   This great victory
raised immensely the Emperor's hopes and increased
his confidence in himself and in his forces.   With
the Lombards subdued he could more easily force the
Pope into submission and put down his pretensions.
Thus, while with regard to the Lombards, who came
offering advantageous conditions of peace, he showed
a determination to accept nothing short of absolute
subjection, he, on the other hand, encouraged the
republican tendencies of Rome, sending the captured
Carroccio as a gift to the senate, and the Romans

placed in the Capitol this trophy from their Cæsar. Gregory fully understood the significance of this act and resented it, but he was not a man easily disheartened ; on the contrary, he seemed fully alive to the risk run by the Church were he to let the Lombards be overpowered without holding out a helping hand. Indeed, from that time the attitude of Gregory became more resolute and more hostile to the Empire, and his alliance with the Guelphs more and more open. Frederick had refused to make conditions with the Lombards, demanding that they should yield at discretion, but they preferred to try again the fortune of war and defend their freedom to the death. This inflexibility on Frederick's part was a great mistake, and thenceforth his star began to wane. The war recommenced, long, fierce, relentless, destined to consume all the forces of the Empire in Italy, but at the same time to introduce new strangers and new tyrannies into a country in which the exuberance of life and some hidden necessity of fate often mixed in too large a measure grief and misfortune with glory.

On the war being renewed, Eccelin da Romano, to whom Frederick had given in marriage a natural daughter of his own, persuaded the Emperor to collect troops for the destruction of Brescia. Siege was laid to the town by Frederick in the summer of 1238, but the courageous city held out against every effort and against atrocities recalling those of his grandfather before Crema, so that after some fruitless months the Emperor was forced to give up the attempt and retire to Cremona. The Guelphs on all sides began to take courage again. Genoa, fearing for her independence, joined the League, and also made peace with Venice through the good offices of the Pope, who now did all he could to isolate and weaken the Emperor.

One reason for the altered attitude of the Genoese was their quarrel with the Pisans about Sardinia, to which both laid claim, while the Church vaunted her rights over it as suzerain, and made use of them in order to have a voice in questions relating to the Mediterranean. Frederick, on his side, put forward pretensions of his own, and, like his grandfather, tried to get a greater influence in the island, not solely for its position respecting Sicily and Africa, but especially to keep it in his hand as a means of alliance with either Pisa or Genoa, when it might serve his turn. Yet, though generally favouring his faithful Pisans, he tried a subtle stroke of policy by marrying his natural son, Enzio, to Adelasia, heiress to the Sardinian principalities of Turri and Gallura, and giving him the title of King of Sardinia. Gregory IX. now decided for open war. Some ambassadors sent to him by the Emperor produced no impression, and on the 20th of March 1239, he thundered forth in the Lateran to terrified listeners a second sentence of excommunication against Frederick, thus heralding in the mortal contest which was to cease only with the utter ruin of the house of Suabia.

The Emperor's wrath was no whit less than the Pope's on hearing of this sentence, which was solemnly announced throughout Europe, while crowds of monks in all directions preached God's anger against the implacable enemy of the Church. Frederick replied to the motives adduced by the Pope with bitter letters, in which he justified himself, and answered the Pope's accusations with others, in which he called him a maker of schisms and discord. Then, turning in an address to the European princes and magnates, he declared that he would not submit to the judgments of a prevaricating and unworthy Pontiff, who condemned him for no other reason but that he had refused to agree to a marriage between a niece of the Pope's and his own son, Enzio. The Pope replied with new invectives, declaring him a liar in the matter of the marriage, which had been proposed by Frederick and declined by him; and then going over the causes of the first excommunication, he related Frederick's persecutions of the clergy in Apulia, his tyranny towards the barons, the support given by him to the Mussulmans, the expedition to the Holy Land prevented by malpractices, and finally Rome encouraged to revolt. Then, in another writing, accusing him openly of heresy and impiety, he says: " This pestilential king maintains that the whole world has been deceived by three impostors, Jesus Christ, Moses, and Mahomet, and affirms, or rather lies, saying that all are mad who believe that God, the Creator of all things, could have been born of a virgin." Thus language grew more and more violent on both sides, and while it rendered all conciliation impossible, it so perverted facts as to make it very difficult for history to distinguish between truth and falsehood.

Throughout 1239 Frederick and his partisans continued fighting against the Lombard Guelphs, with results which differed, but were often unfavourable.

Meanwhile King Enzio, going towards the March of Ancona, made some progress, notwithstanding the armed opposition of Cardinal John Colonna, sent there by Gregory IX., who excommunicated Enzio for invading Church territory. At the same time the Pope laboured indefatigably to strengthen the Guelph party and to excite enmity and rebellion in the kingdom of Sicily, and was apparently also looking round for some prince who might be tempted to try and tear away the crown from the brow of the excommunicated Cæsar. Frederick soon saw that so resolute an enemy must be met by resolute measures, and he marched from Tuscany towards Rome in the spring of 1240, determined to get possession of Gregory's person. Rome, within whose walls there was a large number of imperial partisans, made but a lukewarm show of resistance, and the Pope was in imminent danger, but he found safety in his courageous temper and in the ardent faith which animated him. Having ordained a solemn procession to bear through the city the relics of the cross and the heads of St. Peter and St. Paul, he exposed those precious objects on the high altar in St. Peter's Church, and in burning words invoked the assistance of Heaven for Rome and the Church, both in such grievous peril. The Romans were moved, they crowded round the Pope to take the Cross against the Emperor, and prepared to arm for the defence. Frederick felt that he was not strong enough to assault Rome and retired to Apulia, contenting himself with branding the foreheads of a few of those Roman crusaders who fell into his hands.

Gregory during these occurrences called a council, with the intention of gaining over the principal prelates of Europe, and perhaps of inducing them to join him in deposing the hostile Emperor and in raising up enemies and hindrances to him everywhere. Frederick opposed this project. From the Marche, which he had again invaded, he tried by persuasion and by violence to prevent the bishops from going to Rome, and while he had the Alpine passes watched, he strengthened his navy and called in assistance from his ally Pisa in order to close the way by sea. However, many prelates responded to the Pope's invitation, and meeting at Genoa, set sail for Civita-Vecchia on board Genoese ships, but near Meloria fell in with the ships of Pisa. Here, on the 3rd of May 1241, was fought a fierce battle, in which the Genoese galleys got the worst of it and were taken or sunk. Among the captives were three cardinals and over a hundred bishops and abbots, who were taken to Neapolitan or Sicilian prisons. The council consequently ended in nothing.

The Pope's complaints re-echoed far and near, but Frederick paid no attention to them, and held his prey fast, by which he secured himself against the danger of a council of enemies. At this moment too a terrible peril was hanging over Christendom in the threatened invasion of the Tartars, who, having devastated Russia and Poland, were now descending like an avalanche on the West, and were already on the borders of the Empire. Before this imminent danger it seemed desirable for Pope and Emperor to come to terms, but no agreement was possible,

and as usual each accused the other of being the
cause of the discord.   Frederick raised an army in
Germany which warded off the invaders, but he did
not leave Italy, where success was attending his arms
against the Guelphs of Lombardy and the Romagna.
Determined to subdue Gregory IX., he again approached Rome, and his soldiery spread themselves
over the Campagna, assisted by the warlike Cardinal
Colonna, who had now deserted the Pope.   He took up
his quarters at Grotta Ferrata in view of Rome, and
the city, surrounded as she was, seemed as if she
must open her gates.   But the indomitable man
who had so long opposed him did not undergo the
disgrace of falling into his hands, for on the 21st of
August 1241 he died, almost in sight of his enemy,
as a soldier falls in the breach.   He was an impetuous Pontiff, and, in spite of talent and experience,
not always sufficiently prudent, but he had a high
courage and a manly heart, in which he recalls to us
a later successor, Julius II., who was, however, very
inferior to Gregory in purity of faith and ideality of
purpose.

CHAPTER XIII.

(1241–1250.)

*INNOCENT IV.—IMPLACABLE WAR BETWEEN THE
PAPACY AND THE EMPIRE TILL THE DEATH
OF FREDERICK II.*

AFTER Gregory IX.'s death, Frederick wished to prove
that he respected the liberty of the Church, though
he had held out against the unjust claims of the de-
ceased Pontiff; so he left the neighbourhood of Rome,
and liberated the cardinals who were his prisoners,
on condition that after the election of the Pope they
should return to their captivity. The divided minds
of the cardinals could not agree about the election,
and many of them would have preferred to go away
from Rome for the conclave; but the Romans kept
them shut up, until at last their votes united on the
head of a cardinal of very infirm health, who took the
name of Celestine IV., and died a few days later.
This short pontificate, however, enabled the cardinals
to leave Rome and disperse over the Campagna,
showing themselves more occupied with their own
interests than with those of the Church; and for
nearly two years the Roman see was vacant. Frederick, having made some fruitless overtures for peace,
again overran the Church's territory in the Marche

and Umbria, while in North Italy Eccelin da Romano and the brilliant King Enzio, at the head of the Ghibellines, continued the warfare with the Guelphs, and the country suffered from the ravages of both parties. The want of a Pope, if on one side injurious to the Church, was not either any advantage to Frederick, because the majority of the cardinals were hostile to him, and with them it was difficult to treat definitely, nor had he before him a declared enemy against whom to direct his blows. Therefore he began to insist that the cardinals should stop the scandal of so long a vacancy in such troubled times. The cardinals replied by accusing him of oppression, and demanding the liberation of their colleagues, who had returned to their captivity. Frederick set them at liberty; but the delay continuing, he carried war into the Roman terrritory, and made such havoc that the cardinals had to yield; and being besieged also by the prayers of the rest of Christendom, they met at Anagni on the 24th of June 1243, and selected the Genoese Sinibaldo Fieschi, who took the name of Innocent IV.

Innocent came of a family friendly to the house of Suabia, and he himself had been in the past on friendly terms with the Emperor. On hearing of this election, the imperialists seemed pleased; but it is said that Frederick, with clear intuition of the future, exclaimed, "I have lost a friend, for no Pope will ever be Ghibelline." Even if this is true, he at least outwardly showed satisfaction, ordering that the *Te Deum* should be sung in all the churches throughout the Empire, and sending congratulatory letters to the Pope. It was like a first step in a peaceful direction, and soon after fresh negotiations were entered into, but it was an intricate business. The Pope proposed as conditions that Frederick should liberate the prelates taken at sea, that the matters in which he held himself injured by the Roman Church, or in which he denied having injured her, should be decided by an arbitration of sovereigns, princes, and prelates. The friends of the Holy See, among whom all the Guelphs of Italy must be reckoned, were to be included in the peace, and not in any way to suffer from it. Frederick could not accept this last condition, which Innocent could not give up, and the negotiations came to a stop, so that in the autumn of 1243 the Pope gave notice to the Lombards to hold themselves ready ; that he desired peace with the Emperor, but only on condition of its being extended to all who were faithful to the Church.

The Guelphs responded to the call, encouraged also by the hidden work of Dominicans and Minorites, who were going among the people throughout Italy in spite of Frederick's violent opposition. A sign of this was already given by Viterbo, who being in the hands of the imperialists, entered into a secret alliance with her old enemy Rome, where now the Guelphs were in the ascendant. In August 1243, while the negotiations for peace between Pope and Emperor were still pending, Rome sent soldiers to enable her to rise against the imperial garrison, which was driven back into the citadel, where it made an obstinate resistance. The Pope, asserting that the Roman see had rights over Viterbo, sent further reinforcements, thanks to which the siege of the citadel was carried on with great

vigour.   Frederick in a fury collected a body of men
and rushed to the succour of the beleaguered garrison,
but was repelled by the Romans after having risked
his life, and could only obtain with difficulty that the
garrison should be allowed to leave the citadel alive
and with their arms.   The noise of this event echoed
through Italy and raised the spirits of the Guelphs,
whose leagues grew in numbers and influence.   Many
Ghibelline nobles changed sides and deserted the imperial cause, attracted also no doubt by the gold scattered broadcast by Guelph communes and the Pope.
Germany herself began to vacillate, and Frederick,
unable to abandon the peninsula to Papal intrigues,
determined to guard the Alps with great vigour, in
order to stop all communication between Germany and
the Curia; but his severe measures did little else than
further embitter a quarrel already incurable.

Still the times were heavy and calamitous; there was
famine and death in many parts of Italy, and everywhere a weary need of peace, insomuch that the two
great adversaries were again induced to make a final
effort for an arrangement, which was at last concluded.
The principal conditions were: restitution to the
Roman Church and to her allies of all the territories
seized by the Emperor, liberation of prisoners and
hostages, annulling of all confiscation or ban against
the clergy of the kingdom, pardon to the rebellious
feudatories, and the safeguarding in many ways of the
Lombards' position with regard to the Empire; above
all, the Emperor undertook to declare solemnly to all
European princes that he had resisted the sentence of
excommunication pronounced against him by Gregory

IX., because it had not been duly announced to him, and not from contempt of the Church's authority. On the 31st of March 1244 these conditions were solemnly sworn to in the Lateran by the imperial envoys in the presence of the Pope and of Baldwin, Emperor of Constantinople, and then the Pope announced the Emperor's absolution as being at hand. But people's minds were not at peace. Innocent mistrusted Frederick, who was secretly trying to regain influence in Rome and place it in the hands of his partisans, and he did certainly aim at obtaining the absolution without keeping the conditions. In fact, the whole edifice of this peace soon crumbled and fell. The Pope demanded that Frederick should give their liberty to the prisoners and return the Papal territories before being absolved. Frederick wanted the opposite, and invoked on this difference the arbitration of the kings of France and England, but the Pope did not yield. Yet again all hope of peace vanished, and Innocent, convinced of the wisdom of imitating Gregory IX.'s policy, made up his mind to follow it to the bitter end.

It was not an easy undertaking. It made it necessary to collect the forces of all Christendom against his enemy, so Innocent, adopting once more his predecessor's idea, turned his thoughts to a General Council, but determined to convoke it outside Italy, and where it would be safe from violence. He gave no hint of his intention, and while continuing to treat with Frederick's envoys, he left Rome in June 1244 and betook himself to Civita Castellana, and thence to Sutri. Genoa, secretly informed of the Pope's inten-

tions, sent speedily a fleet to Civita Vecchia, and as soon
as he knew of its arrival, Innocent, with a few trusty
followers, went in disguise on horseback through rough
roads and forests to join it, and on the 7th July
entered his native Genoa in the midst of rejoicings.
Frederick, astonished by this move, guessed what it
meant, and, to induce the Pope to stop, sent the Count
of Toulouse with an offer of immediate submission to
all the conditions, but Innocent held out.   Seeing
that he should not be a welcome guest within the
territory of the French king, who wished to remain
neutral, he decided on going to Lyons, which belonged
by right to the kingdom of Arles, but was in reality a
free and flourishing commune situated most advantageously for the necessary communications.   Though
still weak from a very dangerous illness, Innocent confronted the hardships of a winter journey, and crossing
Mont Cenis, he reached Lyons on the 2nd of December
1244, whence a few days later he convoked the council for the 24th of June of the following year.   The
chief object of the council, according to the Pope, was
to provide for the wretched state of the Holy Land,
and the sad condition of the Latin Empire of Constantinople, to find some remedy against the Tartars,
to examine the differences between the Church and
Frederick, to whom, in his encyclical letter, Innocent
did not give the title of Emperor, and who, he added,
had been cited to appear in person or in the person of
his ambassadors before the council, to reply to the
accusations against him and give suitable satisfaction.

This last object was in truth the one the Pope had
at heart, and for which the council was held, after

some more efforts had been made at a reconciliation, which were as usual unsuccessful on account of insincerity on both sides. Frederick sent the Archbishop of Palermo and the jurist Thaddæus of Sessa to the council to maintain his reasons, while he himself, after holding a great parliament at Verona, in which he hinted at the possibility of his attending the council in person, proceeded to Piedmont to superintend thence the course of events. At the council the English bishops had presented themselves in but small numbers, and this was still more the case with the Germans, for the Pope and the Curia had aroused much mistrust and discontent by their greed and ambition; still about a hundred and forty prelates were present, and those the most hostile to Frederick, against whom very grave accusations were brought of heresy, licentiousness, and Mussulman sympathies. In vain did Thaddæus of Sessa try to defend his master; good or sophistical answers met all his arguments, and every attempt at reply was rejected. At last, on the 17th of July 1245, Innocent, after a long enumeration of all the grievances of the Church, renewed the sentence of excommunication against Frederick, and declared him deposed from the Empire.

Frederick was not disheartened by this prelude of a deadly struggle, yet from that time his chances fell lower and lower, and a mysterious power seemed to shatter every effort he made to recover his old fortune. He immediately sent letters to the princes and clergy of Europe denying the Pope's right to depose him, declaring the council invalid, and the sentence against him to have been inspired by the Pope's personal hate, and based solely on calumny. Frederick exhorted all kings to make common cause with him against the Pontiff, and to be on their guard against the plots of the clergy, whose ambitious and greedy corruption he pointed out. Innocent, for his part, did not keep silence either, and met accusation with accusation, argument with argument, showing that the Pontiff had the power of deposing the Emperor, even though not other kings, sovereigns by hereditary right; and that as to the kingdom of Sicily, he could dispose of it because it was a fief of the Holy See. Specious arguments, which, however, show how once more the course of time had brought a change in the current of thought, and a new idea of public right was arising to free secular power from the authority of the Church, just when this latter was most proudly asserting herself. The European princes in this clashing of rights and claims remained neutral, leaving the two champions to fight it out together.

The first sign of war was the redoubled movement of the Lombard Guelphs, incited to it by the Pope, who helped them largely with the money which he collected from all parts of Christendom and spent without hesitation. The Guelph cities became stronger and more threatening; among the Ghibelline towns there were secret intrigues, intended to give prevalence to the Guelph faction; and the Minorite friars continued to be the principal agents of these intrigues, bearing with indomitable courage even torture and death, which Frederick and his followers often inflicted on them. In Sicily also malcontents began again to stir, and those Saracens who had remained in the

island were especially obnoxious ; while Germany gave
the Emperor more and more anxiety as the Papal
emissaries carried on an active propaganda there, now
in secret, now openly, against the new Nero, the new
Julian, the enemy of the faith and abettor of heresies
and schisms. The Pope, too, aroused the ambitions
of the Electors by inviting them to nominate another
King of the Romans, to whom he promised his support and the crown of the Empire. In vain did the King
of France intercede with the Pope, and in an interview with him at Cluny remind him of the advantage for Christendom of a real peace between the
Church and Empire, and how the expedition of the
Holy Land would be sure of success if joined by
Frederick. The holy ardour of the pious warrior of
France could not kindle the cold nature of this priest,
firm in his belief that only in the complete ruin of her
great enemy could the Church find lasting safety.

Feeling himself entangled in a net of enemies who
reached everywhere and were wily and unscrupulous,
the natural mistrust of Frederick's nature increased ;
and while resolute in resistance, he began, not without reason, to dread everywhere around him treason
and deceit. At the end of the summer of 1245, after
collecting his forces, he again took the field against
the Lombards, and for some months many engagements took place in various places between the leagued
armies and King Enzio or Frederick himself, who
attacked more especially the Milanese ; but these
latter confronted him manfully, and would not let
him pass the Ticino, so that towards November Frederick abandoned the enterprise for the time being, and

went to Tuscany, where he held himself ready to go wherever he was most needed. And indeed in the south a rebellious spirit was abroad; for the Pope, by means of his emissaries and legates, kept alive the irritation of the discontented, excited ambitions, and at least indirectly favoured desertion and treason. In Germany also Innocent laboured in the same sense, renewing his invitation to the Electors to nominate a new king, without any regard for Conrad, who was already King of the Romans, and on whom no sentence of excommunication or deposition rested. Henceforth not only Frederick himself, but all his race were condemned by the holy wrath of the Curia, and for them consideration or recognition of rights no longer existed. At the most, Conrad might have obtained this recognition had he been willing to betray his father, nor were indirect invitations to do so wanting, but he repelled them. The German Electors at first hesitated, unwilling to yield to Papal wishes, but Innocent so incited, flattered, and insisted, that finally a part of them, including the archbishops of Cologne, Mentz, and Triers, gave their votes to Henry of Raspe, Landgrave of Thuringia. Frederick had heaped benefits and honours upon the Landgrave, but he was a man untroubled by scruples, and, taking the title of King of the Romans, he prepared to sustain it by force against Conrad, who attacked him, but was defeated on the banks of the Main on the 25th July 1246, to the great joy of Innocent, who redoubled his efforts to stir up the Germans, and especially to detach from Frederick the most powerful of his friends, Otto, Duke of Bavaria. In this, however, he failed, and even the Duke gave his daughter

Elizabeth in marriage to Conrad, from which union was to spring the last heir of a house doomed to the end to tragic destinies. Conrad again took the field, and in his turn inflicted a thorough defeat on Henry of Raspe, who fled into Thuringia and died soon after. To Innocent was left the difficult task of finding in divided Germany another pretender capable of successfully opposing the Suabians.

From Lyons meanwhile the Pope, by means of his adherents, multiplied Frederick's enemies in Italy, inviting them openly to rebellion, and absolving them from their oath of fidelity. Many plots sprang up, and Frederick, when at Grosseto, had information of a vast network of conspiracy which threatened his throne and life. He was much grieved and angered, for among the conspirators were many whom he had benefited and whom he had held to be proved friends; among others, two sons of the Grand Justiciary Andrea Morra, Andrea Cicala, formerly captain-general in Calabria, Theobald Francesco, who had been podestà at Parma, the family of Sanseverino, and many other influential barons. When discovered, they took refuge in Apulia, but, overtaken and defeated, part of them escaped to Rome, or at least within the southern limits of the Papal state, whence they continued to conspire under the protection of the Pope; part shut themselves up in the castles of Scala and Capaccio, in the territory of Salerno, not hoping to save their life, but determined to sell it dear to the sovereign they had betrayed. Frederick moved to Naples after holding a court at Grosseto, in which he prepared plans for new expeditions in North Italy. He found Scala already taken, and he surrounded Capaccio, which the rebels defended desperately to the end. When it fell, Frederick showed himself merciless, and his passionate nature exacted vengeance, not for the offended majesty of the sovereign only, but for the vile ingratitude with which his benefits had been repaid. Under torture at Naples the chief rebels declared themselves guilty and encouraged by the Pope. Some were instantly hanged or burnt alive or drowned in the sea; but others, after being horribly mutilated and blinded, were dragged as a show and warning from city to city and then cast to the flames. Many wives and daughters of these rebellious barons disappeared for ever and perished in dark prisons.

Frederick complained loudly against Innocent, publicly accusing him of having plotted against his life, but soon after a conspiracy was discovered which aimed at removing Innocent, who then on his side threw all the odium on his enemy. There now existed a strong personal animosity between them, and they calumniated each other both from mistrust and interest, each attributing to the other a misdeed of which neither was guilty. After putting down the rebellions on the mainland, Frederick sent reinforcements to Sicily against the turbulent Saracens, who, on their submitting, were treated indulgently, and carried in great part out of the island to increase the colony of Lucera. Thus Frederick could turn once more to North Italy, and in May 1247 was again at Cremona, where, with Eccelin da Romano and the delegates of the Ghibelline cities, he deliberated regarding the approaching war. At the same time he tried to lull the Guelphs to sleep by spreading the report that negotiations for peace with the Church were on foot and likely to be concluded. Innocent, however, took care to deny this report both in Lombardy and Germany, sending to the former assistance and advice through Cardinal Octavian Ubaldini, while Cardinal Peter Capocci, a clever, determined man, went to Germany to hasten a new election and preach a crusade against the deposed Emperor. Henceforth the banner of the cross was no longer unfurled against the infidels, and the warriors of Christ were openly counselled by the Pope not to think of the Holy Sepulchre for the moment. First must be hewn down this noxious tree which overshadowed the territory sacred to the Church.

Frederick did not shrink before Papal menaces, and as he had once already risen in arms against Gregory IX. and had tried to take him prisoner, so now he thought to conclude the struggle by a daring blow and take possession of this obstinate Pope, in order to force him into a peace, which his long blandishments and promises had failed to persuade him into. Frederick imagined that, once the Pope was caught, he would, in his anxiety to escape, restrain much of his former haughty obduracy, and yield to the lay authority so many concessions as to weaken all future efforts of the spiritual arm. But in this Frederick showed a strange forgetfulness of that agile tenacity which distinguished Papal policy, and he fell into an error already so often committed in the past of history, and to be so often repeated in the future. At any rate, this bold stroke

might at least for the moment succeed and give
some useful results. After collecting an army and
securing the passes of the Alps by means of a few
concessions to the Count of Savoy, Frederick suddenly announced his intention of going to Lyons
to treat personally with the Pope, and of thence
passing into Germany. The King of France, in
some anxiety at this, offered to go and protect the
Pope with an army; but Innocent, fearing lest the
protection should turn into a mediation, recommended
delay and awaited events. He knew well what
he was doing, for when Frederick was on the point
of starting, an unexpected piece of news obliged
him to stop and to change his course of action,
unavoidably, but fatally for his plans. Thanks to
the skilful conduct of Cardinal Gregory of Monte-
longo, a pontifical legate in Lombardy and the soul
of the League, the exiled Guelphs, and among them
the Pope's relatives, succeeded in entering and taking
possession of Parma. Now Parma, from its position,
was quite the citadel of the imperial party, and joined
Tuscany and Central Italy to Piedmont and to the
March of Treviso, so that it was a vital question to
regain it. The Guelphs hastened thither from all
parts, resolved to hold it against the Emperor, who in
person and with an immense army surrounded it in July
1247. He was determined to take the city at whatever cost, but the long and glorious resistance of the
besieged saved the Guelph fortunes in Lombardy. In
vain did the irritated Emperor repeat the horrors with
which his grandfather had tried to break the constancy
of Crema; he met with a constancy which was equal

and more fortunate. Obliged to prolong the siege, he built a new city, where the soldiers could spend the winter in sight of the enemy, and gave it the name of Vittoria. The founding of this city was meant evidently as a promise of Parma's destruction, but the besieged not only took good care of their defences, but on the 18th of February 1248, suddenly falling upon the imperial camp, utterly destroyed it, and set fire to the new city. It was a terrible disaster for Frederick, who, flying and pursued, took refuge in Cremona, leaving his treasures and the imperial insignia in the hands of the Guelphs, who thus at last avenged their own defeat of ten years before at Cortenuova.

For some other months Frederick and his lieutenants tried to retrieve their defeat, but the engagements all went against them, and as ill-luck was followed immediately by desertion, his followers became daily fewer and more lukewarm. He was weakened too by illness and disheartened by the sense of being surrounded by ungrateful traitors. The struggle between Ghibellines and Guelphs lasted very tenaciously in Italy, but it grew more and more to be a struggle between city and city, a strife of local parties against opposing ones, and every day the idea and interests of the Empire were more lost sight of. Frederick, seeing his strength waning, again spoke of peace with the Pope, and the King of France, who was just starting for Palestine, renewed his efforts at mediation, but in vain. The Pope felt that his adversary was now beaten and he continued pitiless. Cardinal Capocci in Germany had orders to proceed resolutely to the destruction of the authority of the

Hohenstaufen, and he executed his task with great firmness and caution. Overcoming many doubts, he succeeded in getting elected as King of the Romans, William, the young Count of Holland, and crowned him himself at Cologne. The Pope sent money to the new king, and wrote warmly in his favour. Among the different parties, the personal ambition of the nobles, and the tendency of many large cities to form free communes, Germany fell into a state of things against which King Conrad's forces did not suffice, and the imperial resources, already so much engaged in Italy, were becoming exhausted. Frederick's distrust of his own strength increased daily, as also his wrath against his enemies and his determination to hold out till the very end.

While Frederick remained in Piedmont, and through opportune concessions was ensuring for himself the Count of Savoy's friendship and making peace with Genoa, Cardinal Rayner, the Papal vicar in Rome, was threatening to invade the Sicilian kingdom and attempt its conquest, so that Frederick felt it needful to hurry to the spot, while the Pope from a distance incited the nobles to rebel. Before moving, however, the suspicion, perhaps the certainty, of another treasonable plot added gall to this already too bitter cup. The matter is enveloped in mystery. One day there was put suddenly in chains at Cremona by Frederick's orders his chancellor, Pier della Vigna, a man who had received so many benefits from him, and for so many years had held the keys of his heart and woven with him the woof of his policy. Soon after, in the prison of Pisa, whither the Emperor had dragged him,

Pier della Vigna killed himself in despair, and this sad suicide inspired one of the most striking passages of the Divine Comedy, in which Dante proclaims him the victim of calumny. At any rate, Frederick held him guilty, and his mistrust was still further increased by the news of rebellion in Sicily, by seeing Eccelin now intent on creating for himself an independent principality without any regard to the imperial interests, and last of all by his doctor's attempt to poison him, of which he publicly accused Innocent IV., and was led to exclaim, " Behold, the honesty of the prince of priests."

In the midst of all this, the embittered sovereign re-entered Apulia towards the spring of 1249, and found the government in great disorder. The excesses of Saracens and Germans, on whom of late years Frederick had specially leaned, the hostile clergy, and the extremely heavy taxes, had disposed people against him, while he, being already in a state of irritation when he arrived, made matters worse by increasing the burdens of his subjects and treating with great severity all who were or whom he suspected of being his enemies. Innocent profited by this discontent, and redoubled his efforts, having the crusade preached against Frederick, and sending from Germany into the Sicilian kingdom the indefatigable Cardinal Capocci, who with great zeal and many intrigues stirred up enemies and rebels against him in every corner. When these were forced into exile, they took refuge close to the borders at Anagni, Subiaco, and Palestrina, where they received succour in money and provisions, and there they awaited the opportunity of stealing back into their country for the ruin of the sovereign.

Meanwhile, things were going on badly in Lombardy, and in the continual warfare between Guelphs and Ghibellines the former had the best of it. Threatened by the Bolognese, who had joined the league of Romagna and of the Po valley, King Enzio determined to free himself from them by a decisive blow, and attacked them on the 29th of May 1249, near a small tributary of the Panaro called the Fossalta, but was defeated and taken prisoner, and so the career of the gallant young King of Sardinia was closed all at once and for ever in the honourable imprisonment in which the Bolognese kept him for the remainder of his life. In vain Frederick entreated, flattered, threatened, in order to obtain his son's freedom, every effort of his was powerless against the determined pride of those burghers. For a year longer the Emperor struggled on amid war, oppression, and conspiracy, but his health no longer could resist the strain. On the 13th of December 1250, in a castle near Lucera, Frederick II. of Hohenstaufen resigned his weary spirit, after an adventurous reign of half a century, which was full of contradictions in its fortunes and vicissitudes, in its virtues and its crimes, as was the character of the prince and of the times in which he lived. Heir to a principle now wearing out, yet of a subtle and pliable nature, he felt the influence of the transformations taking place in the world around him, but could not always trace their path. With Frederick II., although he was more an Italian than a German Emperor, every vital element of the Empire in Italy faded away.

CHAPTER XIV.

(1250-1258.)

*INNOCENT IV. AND FREDERICK II.'S SUCCESSORS,
CONRAD AND MANFRED.*

FRÉDERICK II. had, in his will, left to Conrad, King of
the Romans, the thrones of Germany and Italy, and in
case of Conrad's dying childless, his brother Henry,
son of Isabella of England, and still a child, was to
succeed him.   To his grandson Frederick, son of the
rebel Henry, he left the duchy of Austria.   Manfred,
fruit of the Emperor's amours with Bianca Lancia,
and later made legitimate by a subsequent marriage,
was created Prince of Taranto and viceroy of Sicily
during the absence of Conrad.   His natural sons,
Frederick of Antioch and Enzio, were not mentioned
in the will.

The merciless hatred of the Popes formed part of
the inheritance of Frederick's sons.   Innocent IV.,
who publicly rejoiced over the Emperor's death, instantly set to work, and hoped to succeed in speedily
annihilating this "race of vipers," which he had
doomed to destruction.   But Frederick's sons possessed all the old Suabian vigour and the struggle
continued.   Discord and anarchy were rife in Ger-

many and Italy, but in the former Conrad held his own against his rival William of Holland, while in Italy the young Manfred, suddenly revealing himself as a statesman and warrior, saved his brother's kingdom. Manfred was but eighteen when his father died; he was fair, handsome, and of graceful presence; his intellect was ready and versatile, and at his father's court he had grown up fond of arts and letters and anxious to distinguish himself in arms, generous, affable, firm in chararcter but lax in morals, and caring little for religion. On his father's death he seized the regency, while Cardinal Capocci, following the Pope's orders, stirred up the kingdom and incited many cities to rebellion, among which Barletta, Capua, and Naples, and nearly all the country between the Garigliano and the Volturno. Manfred was undismayed; though without money, he collected soldiers, regained Andria and Foggia, and marching rapidly on Barletta, tried to take it by storm. The citizens defended themselves with such a hail of stones and arrows from the walls that the assailants hesitated, till Manfred flung himself to the front, and the soldiers, encouraged by the intrepidity of their youthful leader, followed him, and Barletta was taken. Nor was it long before the kingdom was subdued, with the exception of a few cities like Capua and Naples, against which Manfred made some fruitless attempts.

The Pope meanwhile thought it better for his object to leave Lyons and return to Italy; but first he sought an interview with William of Holland, whose election he confirmed, and renewing his anathemas, he had the crusade preached against Conrad in Germany. On his return to Italy in the spring of 1251, he stopped at Genoa and Milan, and in many towns of Lombardy, received everywhere with great honour, under which, however, a certain feeling of mistrust was ill concealed. During his journey he tried everywhere, but with little result, to strengthen the Guelphs and reconcile the Ghibellines ; nor did he hesitate to try to gain the friendship of Eccelin da Romano, who, however, conscious that his strength depended on the Ghibellines, held out against the Pope's blandishments. Innocent aimed at entering Rome, but he thought it prudent not to trust himself too hastily to a city which had always shown such fickleness and unfriendliness towards the Popes. He stopped therefore at Perugia.

But he was not the only one to seek Italy, which became the chief theatre of events, for a few months later Conrad of Hohenstaufen also betook himself thither. Seeing that the present state of Germany allowed of no decisive action either on his own or his adversary's part, Conrad resolved to go and make sure of the kingdom of Sicily, and thwart the Papal designs by rousing the Ghibelline party in Italy. He left in Germany his queen, Elizabeth, who was near her confinement, reached Verona in the November of 1251, held in the neighbouring Goito a diet, which was attended by Eccelin and the principal Ghibelline leaders, and took counsel with them ; then, to avoid hindrances, embarked with his troops near Trieste, and on reaching the Neapolitan coast, disembarked at Siponto, where Manfred was waiting as if to hand over to him the kingdom he had saved. At first Conrad showed great gratitude to his brother, heaped honours

upon him, and appointed him high constable of the
realm, but soon there came a change. Of a sullen and
haughty disposition, a complete stranger to the country
he came to rule, Conrad could hardly be expected to
look favourably on the popular young prince, full of
grace and courage, who had already taken so pro-
minent a part in state affairs, and naturally attracted
attention and sympathy. Gradually, under one pretext or another, he deprived him of almost all the fiefs
left him by his father, and sent out of the kingdom
Manfred's relatives on his mother's side, who were
rich in possessions and followers. Manfred made no
resistance, and continued to serve his brother faithfully,
hiding any vexation he may have felt.

Conrad—to whom a son, Conradin, was born in Germany in March 1252—made an effort to reconcile the
Pope by sending ambassadors to Perugia, who were
received, but their proposals were rejected, so that the
hatred between the two parties grew more bitter. As
in the times of Frederick, both camps began again to
hurl horrible accusations at each other ; and Conrad,
accused by the Pope of poisoning his nephew, Frederick,
Duke of Austria, believed rather that he himself was
in danger from Innocent, and consequently increased
in severity against the Papal partisans, and was confirmed in his determination to quell with fire and
sword the ever-spreading rebellion. Collecting all
his forces, and accompanied by Manfred, he subdued
the rebellious towns very sternly, then approached
the walls of Naples, resolved to take the town at
any cost. The Neapolitans, dreading Conrad's severity,
were equally resolved to resist ; and the Pope, seeing

how vital the taking of Naples was to his enemy, encouraged the besieged and tried to divide the besieger's forces by creating difficulties for him elsewhere. The Papal emissaries laboured without rest in Lombardy and Germany to change Conrad's adherents into enemies; but Conrad did not for this leave the walls of Naples, which resisted long and desperately, and only after nine months' siege surrendered, with entreaties for mercy to Conrad, who proved merciless. This victory, and the severity which followed it, ensured the possession of the kingdom, and Conrad was soon able to return to Germany, while the Pope sought new means of opposing him, and desired to find some foreign prince who would undertake the conquest of Sicily. He entered into treaty in England, first with Richard of Cornwall, then with Edmund, son of Henry III., to induce one of them to accept the investiture; but these negotiations failed for the time, and so did others with Charles of Anjou, brother of the French king. This greedy and ambitious prince was longing to assume the rich Sicilian crown, but he could not accept the invitation. King Louis was in the East, the French Crusaders had been unfortunate, the country was impoverished, and the times were too unsettled for an arduous and costly expedition. Innocent renewed his solicitations in England, and meanwhile betook himself to Rome, where he was pretty well received by the Romans, who, however, under the rule of a powerful and resolute senator, the Bolognese Brancaleone d'Andalò, were maintaining their municipal independence, and did not practically recognise the Pontiff as

their prince.   Other attempts of Conrad's to reconcile
the Pope not only failed, but ended in a sentence of
excommunication.   The Pope's courage had greatly
increased, because Henry III. had consented that his
son Edmund should accept the investiture of Sicily, a
consent which was more easily obtained owing to the
death of Henry, the brother of Conrad and nephew on
the mother's side to the English king, who would have
been unwilling to usurp his nephew's eventual rights.
It is also said that the Papal emissaries made skilful
use of calumny, insinuating that Conrad had poisoned
his brother; and certainly the accusation spread among
the Guelphs and in the Curia, but it was based on
hostility, and had no foundation in fact.

While the Pope was redoubling his efforts and intrigues to carry Edmund into Sicily, an unexpected
occurrence appeared to modify his intentions.   When
preparing to return to Germany, Conrad of Hohenstaufen died, after a very short illness, on the 21st
of May 1254.   He was twenty-six years of age, and
in difficult circumstances he had proved himself a very
resolute prince and courageous warrior, but had no
opportunity of showing whether he also possessed
statesmanlike qualities.   He left as heir of his contested realms the child Conradin, who was in Germany
with his mother Elizabeth, and appointed as regent the
Marquis Berthold of Hohenburg, instructing him to
seek reconciliation with the Pope.   To Manfred he
merely recommended his son's interests, without giving
him any special title or position in the kingdom of
Sicily, which thus remained in the hands of a German
soldier unversed in its affairs and disliked by the people.

Berthold of Hohenburg soon found the regency a difficult task, and after vain efforts at reconciliation with the Pope, he ended by giving up the reins of government to Manfred, who accepted them with at least seeming hesitation. Innocent had drawn nearer to the boundaries of the kingdom by taking up his residence at Anagni, whence he sent orders on all sides to collect troops. Seeing that Manfred was weak, without money, suspected by the German barons and by some of the Sicilians, who were secretly drawn into the opposition by Papal emissaries, Innocent, neglecting the interests of the English prince with whom he was in treaty, sought rather to hasten himself the conquest of the Sicilian kingdom, with the intention perhaps of bestowing it later under conditions of greater vassalage. Manfred, on his side, was conscious of the difficulty of his position, and felt that his only safety lay in temporising; for the Pope was old and infirm and might not live long. He therefore offered him the guardianship of Conradin and the regency, declaring himself disposed to receive him and give into his hands the strong places of the realm, with due regard, however, to his own and his nephew's rights.

It is not easy to say how far Manfred's offer was genuine, but the Pope seemed very much pleased with it, and he soon freed the prince from excommunication, confirmed him in the possession of all his fiefs, including those which Conrad had taken from him, and appointed him apostolic vicar over a large part of the kingdom; but touching Conradin he held himself more in reserve. What the astute Pontiff also wanted

was time to cross the frontier without opposition.
Manfred went to meet him at Ceprano, and on his
entrance into the kingdom at the bridge over the
Garigliano paid him liege homage, leading his palfrey
by the bridle, and together they went to San Germano.
Thence after a few days they proceeded to Teano,
while the Papal troops, under the Cardinal of St. Eus-
tachius, went on to take possession of many important
fortresses. Repeated were the demonstrations of devotion on one side and benevolence on the other, but
under these lying appearances a reality of hatred and
intrigue was smouldering, and Manfred soon became
aware that the Pope was in truth master of the realm.
Innocent, gradually feeling himself stronger, began to
cool in his behaviour towards Manfred, and the increasing ambiguity of his conduct showed a disposition to separate Manfred's last followers from him and
to flatter his enemies. Among these latter there was
then at Teano a baron, Burrello of Anglona, who had
received benefits from both Manfred and King Conrad,
but was now disputing one of Manfred's fiefs on the
pretext that the Pope had granted it to him. The
Pope, on being questioned, replied vaguely, not daring
to do the prince an open injustice, yet unwilling to
favour him, so that Manfred, more and more irritated
and suspicious, left the Papal court, on the plea of
going to meet the Marquis Berthold of Hohenburg,
who was on his way. And indeed he was anxious to
see him, and prevent him, an ambitious and discontented man, from throwing himself into the Pope's
arms, and thus destroying the last chance of preserving
the kingdom to the Suabian dynasty.

On leaving Teano, at a short distance from the town, Manfred and his followers met Burrello in a narrow and dangerous pass, as if the latter were there in ambush, or at least in an attitude of defiance. Manfred's soldiers flung themselves on those of the baron, and he took to flight, but was followed and killed, against Manfred's wish, according to the chroniclers on his side—by his express order, according to the Guelphs. What is certain is, that after Burrello's death Manfred felt that he must hasten on, as probably he would be followed by the Papal troops. Wherever he went there was danger, especially in the Terra di Lavoro, which was now wholly occupied by the Pope's soldiers, where the people were frightened, and he might at any moment be taken prisoner. After many adventures he reached Acerra, and thence asked for an interview with Berthold of Hohenburg, who, however, avoided him, and proceeded straight to the Papal court, where he pretended to join the envoy sent by Manfred to excuse the death of Burrello, but in reality seems to have worked on the Pope in a contrary sense. Manfred's uncle, the faithful Galvano Lancia, who was at the court to further his interests, sent warning to his nephew, and advised him to go to Lucera, where the Saracen troops would protect him. Manfred followed the advice, and leaving Acerra, he again started on his dangerous march, first as far as Venosa, whence on the 1st of November 1254, almost alone, by difficult paths and on a rainy night, he left for Lucera. In the morning he was in sight of the walls, which he approached with only three of his most intimate followers, and telling the guards of one of the

gates who he was, asked that they would let him in.
The guards had not the keys of the gate, but burst it
open, and raising him on their shoulders, bore him in
triumph through the city.   He took the command of
his faithful Saracens, and found at Lucera a nucleus of
troops wherewith to restore the fortunes of his family.
The turn of the tide was again favourable, for at
Lucera he also found much treasure, and was able to
form a vigorous army, with which he went towards
Foggia, and took it after defeating Otto of Hohenburg, Berthold's brother.   This defeat terrified the
cardinal legate, who was encamped at Troia with the
mass of the Papal army, which fled in great disorder to
Naples, whither the Papal court had moved.

At Naples the fugitives found that Innocent IV.
had died on the 7th of December 1254, and the cardinals, out of heart on seeing the army arrive in such
disorder, were hardly to be prevailed upon by Berthold
of Hohenburg not to fly from Naples, but to remain
there and elect the new Pope, who was the Cardinal of
Ostia, Rainald, of that same family of Segni which
had already given the Popes Innocent III. and Gregory IX.   He took the name of Alexander IV., and at
first showed more moderation with regard to Manfred,
whose troops had various successes over the Papal
ones, which were led by Cardinal Ubaldini, suspected
later of secretly favouring the prince.   Meanwhile,
some envoys sent from Germany by Elizabeth, the
mother of Conradin, and by his uncle the Duke of
Bavaria, confirmed Manfred as guardian of the boy-
king and regent of the kingdom, and went to the
Pope with proposals of peace.   The Pope did not

seem averse to it, and during the negotiations concluded a truce; but the cardinal legate broke it by
moving his troops in such a way as to interrupt Manfred's communication with Lucera, on which Manfred
indignantly resumed hostilities and inflicted a tremendous defeat on the pontifical troops. The Cardinal,
reduced to extremities, proposed an agreement. The
Pope was to recognise Conradin and Manfred, and to
invest them with all the kingdom except the Terra di
Lavoro, which was to become a direct possession of the
Church. Manfred accepted the conditions, allowed
the legate to retire with his soldiers, and granted a
full pardon to Berthold of Hohenburg, and to the
other barons who had fought against him and now
returned to their allegiance.

When the Cardinal Ubaldini submitted these terms
to the Pope, there were great outcries in the Curia; the
cardinal was accused of betraying the Guelph interests,
and the terms were rejected. The negotiations with
the King of England had been again more actively
resumed, and Henry had promised to undertake an
expedition into Sicily in favour of his son Edmund,
and settled with the Holy See the conditions of the
investiture; but in reality he never was able to keep
his promise. Manfred, seeing that the Pope declined
the proposed agreement, and that in Germany, after
the death of William of Holland, there was a strong
opposition to Conradin's election, felt that the time had
come to act with energy. On the 2nd of February
1256 he held a large parliament at Barletta, conferred
fiefs and important posts on the most faithful of his
barons, among whom were his relatives Galvano and

Frederick Lancia, and on discovering fresh treachery on the part of Berthold of Hohenburg and other nobles, he had them arraigned and condemned. Thus secured, and while the Lancia made successful expeditions in Calabria and Sicily, reducing them to obedience, Manfred advanced into the Terra di Lavoro, and fighting indefatigably for the whole of 1256, regained the kingdom with the exception of a few castles here and there.

Thus the Papacy found itself again in troubled waters, and its difficulties did not only arise south of Rome, but extended to the whole peninsula. Rome herself was unsettled, nor was there much hope of succour from beyond the Alps. The Ghibellines of Central and Northern Italy, admiring the successful determination of Manfred, began to regard him as their leader and to lose no time in renewing their relations with him. Alexander IV. felt the danger, and as he had no other weapons, he tried to break, by a sentence of excommunication, the new ties which were forming, and in April 1257, at Viterbo, he hurled it against Manfred; but the bolt fell harmlessly. On all sides Manfred's adherents among the Italian Ghibellines were increasing. Venice entered into alliance with him, and he strengthened his position by overcoming forcibly the last efforts of resistance, and then making opportune concessions to the conquered, so that in the spring of 1258 he re-entered Palermo as the restorer of the Suabian monarchy. This young prince had done great things in a few short years of untiring activity. He had saved the kingdom for a heartless brother, who had returned his devotion with ingratitude. On his brother's death, he alone, without assistance or support, had again conquered and saved the kingdom. Amid diplomatic wiles, amid the dangers and bitterness of flight, in the proud hour of battle, he had always borne himself as a king. And now that the sceptre was safe in his hands, was he, who, after all, like every Hohenstaufen, was ambitious and unscrupulous—was he to give it up to a child born and brought up under other skies, unknown to the people, and hardly knowing the existence of a kingdom which to Manfred meant glory and life? Nor were other excuses wanting to satisfy an ambitious conscience. The times were difficult, the Ghibelline party needed a strong arm to guide it. Perhaps in this way he would later be better able to help Conradin in Germany. Frederick I. had been chosen king instead of a child, Philip of Suabia had taken the place of Frederick II.; it seemed almost traditional in the family for the uncle to supplant the nephew. A false report was suddenly spread throughout Sicily that Conradin was dead, and without waiting to verify it, Manfred, giving way to the instances of his courtiers, was crowned king at Palermo in August 1258; but the throne which he was thus usurping was to be torn away from him by another act of usurpation.

CHAPTER XV.

(1258–1266.)

THE POPES BRING CHARLES OF ANJOU INTO ITALY—
DEATH OF MANFRED AT BENEVENTO.

WHEN Manfred assumed his nephew's crown at Palermo, he broke the ties which bound him to Germany
and became naturally a national king, just at the
moment when the feudal Germanic idea of the Empire
was declining in Italy, and the Ghibellines needed
some new banner round which to rally. Hence the
fame of Manfred increased rapidly throughout the peninsula, and his growing power soon became a terror
and an object of ever-increasing hatred to the Papacy,
to which the Guelphs could give but little real support, being mere partisans, whose forces were falling
to pieces because no common national interest united
them any more in one strong bond. Germany was
in complete anarchy between two shadows of kings-
elect, Richard of Cornwall and Alfonso of Castile, and
could no longer exert the least influence in Italian
affairs. The Guelphs themselves in Lombardy began
to draw near the new king of Sicily. Under these
circumstances, one might have expected the Pope to
have attempted a reconciliation with Manfred, and, by

winning him over, make him a Guelph and an instru-
ment for Papal purposes. But it would have been a
difficult experiment, and would have needed a greater
and more daring spirit than that of Alexander IV.
The series of powerful Popes who had offered so grand
a resistance to the Suabian Emperors had closed with
Gregory IX., and there followed now a series of rather
commonplace men—men of a certain ability, but without any breadth of ideas or depth of feeling. On the
other hand, the fear lest Manfred, who had always been
hostile to the Church, should gain influence, and perhaps direct sovereignty, north of Rome, was by no
means irrational; and the Curia turned all its subtle
intelligence to opposing him, and did succeed in separating the Guelphs from him, so that Manfred, by the
force of circumstances, ended by following the natural
instinct of his race, and placed himself at the head of
the Ghibellines.

Order again flourished in the Sicilian realm, and
Manfred combined with state cares the joyous life of a
youthful court, where talents and beauty, love of pleasure and of art, lent their brilliancy. On the death of
his first wife, Beatrice of Savoy, Manfred married the
Greek princess Helen, daughter of the despot of Epirus,
thus allying his kingdom with the East. Meanwhile
the Emperor Baldwin was asking for help for the Latin
Empire in the East, which was tottering, and in
order to obtain it tried to make peace between the
Popes and Manfred. This effort failed, the Pope
having put as his first condition the destruction of the
colony of Lucera and the departure of the Saracens,
who were Manfred's chief and surest support against

all Papal attacks. As usual, after vain attempts at peace, recourse was again had to arms; and, under colour of other expeditions, Manfred's soldiers, led by the Genoese Percival d'Oria, entered the March of Ancona. The Ghibellines on all sides invoked Manfred all the more, since Eccelin da Romano, till then the strongest support of their party in Northern Italy, had been vanquished and killed, and the power of his family for ever destroyed.

But the destruction of the house of Romano had not sufficed to change the party fortunes; and while throughout Lombardy the small wars of faction continued, in Tuscany the exiled Ghibellines tried to re-enter their native Florence. From Siena they sought to collect partisans on every side, and appealed to Manfred for assistance, assuring him that by destroying the Guelphs in Florence he would have uprooted Guelphism throughout Tuscany. At first Manfred, knowing the great strength of the Guelphs in Central Italy, received the invitation coldly, only sending to Siena a hundred German knights, who were quite insufficient for the enterprise. But in an encounter with the Florentines these knights were overpowered by superior numbers, and the imperial eagle was trailed ignominiously through the streets of Florence. Manfred could not overlook the insult offered to his banner, and sent a strong body of cavalry to join the Ghibellines. The Guelphs also on their side were in great force. At Montaperti, on the banks of the Arbia, there was fought with great obstinacy on the 4th of September 1260, one of the most memorable battles of that age, which opened the gates of Flor-

ence to the victorious Ghibellines. It was then that
the Ghibelline leaders in council proposed to utterly
exterminate Florence, and the hateful suggestion
would have been followed if the magnanimous Farinata degli Uberti, who had been the leading spirit
among the exiles, had not, alone and openly, defended
the city which no bitterness of banishment could make
him hate. Thus Farinata preserved for its glorious
future this fair city of the Muses.

The victory of Montaperti had raised Manfred to
a high position in Italy. The Ghibellines, rallying
closer round him, prevailed now in most of the Tuscan
towns, giving little heed to the excommunication pronounced by Alexander against Siena and against every
one who in Tuscany or Lombardy entered into alliance
with the victorious prince, now apparently master of
the peninsula. It behoved the Church, if she meant to
persevere in her policy, to take vigorous measures,
and hence, to those who held this view, the death of
Alexander IV. did not appear inopportune. To him
succeeded, on the 29th of August 1261, a Frenchman, Urban IV., a man of great energy, who was determined to fight untiringly for the Church's interests
in Italy. From Italy herself Urban IV. could hope
nothing, so he turned to his native France, where an
ambitious prince and a chivalrous and often poor
nobility were likely to respond to his call from a
desire for adventures and wealth. Delay would be
fatal. Manfred's adherents were daily increasing,
and in Rome they were seeking to elect him senator
in opposition to Richard of Cornwall, the candidate
of another party. Also, in spite of the Pope's oppo-

sition, Manfred's daughter Constance was about to marry Peter, heir to the crown of Aragon. Urban, after renewing at Viterbo his predecessor's anathemas against Manfred, sent an envoy to the French court to treat secretly the question of investing Charles of Anjou with the kingdom of Sicily. The Pope repeated the proposals already made in vain by Innocent IV., but at a more favourable moment, for the condition of France had much improved in the interval. Louis IX., as if divining the ascendancy France was about to take in European politics, began to listen, though still with hesitation, to the invitations of the Pope, who did all he could to set at rest the King's scruples regarding the lawfulness of an undertaking which not only injured Manfred but was contrary to the prior claims of Conradin and of Edmund of England. While these negotiations were pending, Manfred, who had some inkling of what was going on, tried to make friends again with the Pope and offered terms of peace; nor did Urban, doubtful as he yet was of the decision of France, immediately decline them, but let matters drag on.

The negotiations in France being actively pushed, at last succeeded, and Urban's envoys, having obtained from the English king the surrender of his son Edmund's rights, succeeded in conquering Louis IX.'s hesitation, and they began to discuss the conditions under which Charles of Anjou would receive the investiture and would undertake to conquer the kingdom. Of virile and tenacious ambition, greedy of gold and power, possessing prudence and resolution, and untroubled by scruples or feelings of compassion,

Charles of Anjou had the natural gifts necessary for gaining a kingdom, and, having gained it, for keeping it. In August 1263, while they were still discussing the conditions of the investiture, Charles, taking keen advantage of the dissensions in Rome, prevailed on the Romans to elect him senator of the city. He thus got a footing in Italy independently of the Papal invitation, and while diminishing Manfred's influence in Rome, he also guarded against the possibly overweening pretensions of his benefactor in the future. Urban grew uneasy, protested, showed even some hesitation respecting the investiture, so that the negotiations were delayed. But Manfred meanwhile was more and more threatening; the Guelphs, aroused by the Pope's admonitions, needed a leader; grave events pended in Europe and the East, and all these considerations shook Urban's resistance, while Charles persevered. At last Urban gave way on Charles's promise to retain only for a time the senatorial dignity.

These difficulties being smoothed over, Charles sent on ahead an officer to act for him as senator, promising to be soon in Rome himself, and then collected the army which was to be led by him to conquest. Manfred, seeing the danger approaching, thought to anticipate it by sending large bodies of troops into the Patrimony and the Marche, where many encounters took place with the followers of Urban, who did not cease to preach a crusade against the enemy. And indeed Manfred at that time was a formidable opponent, notwithstanding the hopes placed on the invader. At Rome an effort made by his partisans to get possession of the city had failed, but in the rest of Italy the Ghibellines were holding their heads up, and were able to oppose the march of the Angevin. An imposing array of ships guarded the Maremma coast, and the mouth of the Tiber had been barred to prevent the access of Charles's galleys, should he choose the sea. The Pope himself, surrounded on every side and no longer able to remain in the neighbourhood of Rome, had retired to Perugia, where he was giving his attention to settling the last difficulties of his negotiations with Charles, when he died on the 2nd of October 1264. On the same day a comet disappeared from the skies after two months, during which its presence had gloomily agitated the whole of Italy with presentiments of war and misfortune.

For more than four months the cardinals in conclave could come to no agreement. The Italians would have wished to change policy and join Manfred, but the French party were determined to follow the path traced by Urban IV., and they were superior in numbers. So a Frenchman was elected, Guy, cardinal of St. Sabina and archbishop of Narbonne. Before taking priest's orders he had been a lawyer in office at the court of Louis IX., was devoted to the royal family of France, and knew them thoroughly. He took the name of Clement IV., pushed on rapidly the treaty with Charles of Anjou, and the expedition was definitely decided on. Again the crusade against Manfred was preached with great fervour and promises of spiritual rewards; the Papal legates in France and England extracted all the money they could for the purpose, soldiers thronged from all quarters, led by brave and adventurous barons, who gazed with avidity on the country rich in spoil to which fortune called them. The army collected at Lyons before passing the Alps. Charles with a thousand chosen lances preceded them, and took ship at Marseilles. As soon as he had sailed, the wind rose in fury, and the stormy sea saved the fortunes of the royal adventurer. The Sicilian admiral, who was guarding the Tuscan coast, had taken to the open, fearing to be dashed on the rocks, and convinced that Charles also would not dare to approach the shore, with the almost certain risk of shipwreck. But Charles had gone forward trusting in his star, and now, tossed on the waves and separated from his other ships, he reached the Roman coast, landed almost alone near Ostia, and was soon met and welcomed by the Guelphs of Rome, who conducted him with all honours to the monastery of St. Paul. Joined there by his followers, he entered Rome in triumph on the 23rd of May 1265, and on the 21st of June took formal possession of his senatorial dignity in the Capitol. A week later, from the hands of cardinals sent expressly by the Pope from Perugia, he received in the Lateran the investiture of the kingdom and swore liege homage to the Pontiff.

Manfred meanwhile was prepared to defend himself, and before Charles's arrival in Rome the Sicilian soldiers had had an advantage over the officer who was filling the senatorial dignity for Charles, and this advantage had seemed of happy augury. But the indefatigable and invisible activity of the Pope and his emissaries acted as a dissolvent in Manfred's army and throughout the kingdom, and even where gold could not corrupt nor spiritual terrors appal, uncertainty as to the result produced a chilling effect. After entering the Campagna, Manfred had hoped to make himself master of Rome, and stop the war in its beginnings; but Charles was both prudent and vigorous, and Manfred recognised that he could not leave his kingdom for long if he would keep it loyal and ready for war. The summer of 1265 passed in encounters of small importance, and towards November French troops from Provence began to pour over the Alps. Manfred's principal hope lay in the Ghibellines of Northern and Central Italy, as their resistance might bar the way to Charles's army, or at least so weaken it as to make it harmless; but as in the Sicilian realm so in the north, the Pope was exerting himself to smooth the way for the invaders, who met with little resistance, and in the first days of 1266 joined in Rome their leader, who on the feast of the Epiphany was crowned solemnly in the Vatican by the Pope's legates as king of Sicily and Apulia.

Thus blessed by the Church, he proceeded against the excommunicated prince, who awaited him resolved to resist, but doubtful of those around him. Charles advanced rapidly, preceded by a great reputation. The first line of defence was on the Garigliano; but the traitor Richard, Count of Caserta, Manfred's brother-in-law, retired without striking a blow, and left the road open to San Germano, which was taken, and in the sack of the unhappy city the victors had a foretaste of the joys and advantages of conquest. Without losing time, Charles arrived by forced marches at Benevento, where Manfred was, and the two armies found themselves face to face. The fatal hour of a decisive battle had sounded, and on both sides there was nothing left but to conquer or to die; but in Manfred's ranks treason and presentiments of evil were abroad, and the prince was advised by some to fly and wait for better times. "Rather die here like a king to-day than go forth as a fugitive and beggar to a foreign land," was his answer, and he kept his word. It was the 26th of March 1266. Long and fiercely raged the battle that day in the plains of Benevento, and Manfred was beaten, but did not leave the battlefield. Followed by a few faithful friends, the brave and handsome knight flung himself among his victorious enemies and found a royal death. In the plain, which was strewn with the dead, Manfred long lay unrecognised, while the victors filled the streets of Benevento with horrors and bloodshed. At last the fair corpse, anxiously sought for by Charles, was found, and sadly was the wail repeated, "Dead is Manfred! dead is Manfred!" By order of Charles some captive barons were taken to identify him, and a contemporary chronicler exclaims, "Oh! oh! with what profusion of tears those trembling ones raise the recovered corpse of Manfred, and kiss their lord's hands and feet! 'This is the innocent one who has died for us; this is he who loved us unto death.' And near his body was found that of Theobald Annibaldi, who had always followed Manfred's footsteps in the battle. Manfred's dead body being taken thence, it was placed near a ruined church, and over it, to do it honour, the French heaped a large heap of stones." Thus outside consecrated ground, yet near a church and in honoured sepulchre, lay Frederick's excommunicated son, but not even

there was there peace for his bones, which later were
removed by the priestly hatred of the Bishop of Cosenza
to an unknown spot near the banks of a river, where
" still the rain falls and the winds beat upon them."
The Queen Helen and Manfred's children were taken,
and languished in the prisons of the conqueror, who
was as pitiless towards them as Henry VI. had been
to Queen Sibilla and the children of Tancred. All
bowed down in homage or in cowardice before Charles
of Anjou, who was now lord of the realm.

CHAPTER XVI.

(1266–1268.)

THE LAST OF THE HOHENSTAUFEN.

" O King Manfred! We did not know thee alive, and now we bewail thy death! We thought thee a rapacious wolf among the sheep of this kingdom, but now in comparison to the present rule, which with our usual inconstance we so anxiously longed for, we recognise in thee an innocent lamb. We already feel that thy commands were gentle because we are tasting the harsh ones of this other. We used to complain that thou tookest from us a part of our substance, but now all our possessions, and what is worse, even our persons, are the prey of these foreigners." [1] Thus did the people in a short time begin to lament Manfred's fall and the oppression of their new lord, who, born to subdue and inspire terror, had promptly secured his dominion in the conquered realm, but could not so soon erase the memory of a chivalrous and gracious prince. The discontented people were nursing their

---

[1] SABA MALASPINA, *Rerum Sicularum Historia*, iii. 17, ap. MURATORI, *R. I. S.*, viii. 832. It is worth noticing that this contemporary chronicler, from whom also we have quoted the words relating to Manfred's death in the foregoing chapter, belonged to the Guelph party and had a post at the Papal court.

anger, and the Suabian party were aware of this and founded hopes upon it. But since the battle of Benevento the Guelphs had greatly prevailed throughout Italy, and their eyes were already fixed on Charles of Anjou as their champion, and they trusted in him to help them to subdue the Ghibellines, who, though overpowered, did not, especially in Tuscany, give up the contest. Charles rejoiced at this disposition in the Guelphs and encouraged it, for his ambitious hopes on one side extended beyond the banks of the Garigliano, anxious as he was for influence and authority over the whole of Italy, and on the other indulged in visions of such power in the East as the Normans and Suabians had already exercised.

This vast ambition was not altogether unsuspected by the Pope, who was thoroughly conversant with Charles's character long before this Sicilian expedition, and he tried in the interests of the Church to restrain its ardour. He had not called on Charles to overturn Manfred in order to erect a strong Guelph despotism in the place of the Ghibelline, but to have a devoted champion invested with the kingdom to which the Church laid claim. A certain sense of suspicion and discontent, and a certain wish to interfere even in the internal policy of the new prince, soon showed themselves in the letters from the Pope, to whom Charles's excessive severity towards his new subjects was displeasing, as well as his extremely despotic and rapacious proclivities. Even if Clement's warm and sincere zeal for the Church's interests led frequently to his passing over many things, this very zeal also made him often suspicious of the intentions of Charles and careful not to let himself be overborne by them. Reminding him of the former conditions, he asked Charles to give up his office as senator of Rome, and Charles at last was obliged unwillingly to do so. Clement thought by that to regain possession of Rome ; but the Romans would not bow to the Papal authority ; the democratic party in the city joined the Ghibellines and got the best of it, and after various vicissitudes a new and unlooked-for senator was elected—Henry of Castile, brother of Alfonso the Wise, the titular King of the Romans. Exiled from home, after exhibiting much prowess in Africa against the Moors, and having many adventures, Henry chanced to come to Italy in search of fortune. At the court of Charles, who owed him money, he was received with fair words and with nothing else. At Viterbo from the Pope he tried to obtain the investiture of the kingdom of Sardinia, to which he laid claim, but did not find him favourable ; and when he discovered that Charles was working secretly against him, he determined to have his revenge. Making friends with the Romans, he obtained the senatorial dignity, and lost no time in exercising it vigorously against the clerical party, to the great joy of the Ghibellines, whose hopes rose on meeting with his support.

In Tuscany especially these hopes were more lively, and caused anxiety to the Guelphs, who naturally turned to Charles of Anjou ; and even the Pope himself, after the unfortunate result of depriving him of the senatorial dignity, again had recourse to him, in spite of some lingering mistrust. The remnants of the army defeated at Benevento had taken refuge in the Ghibelline cities of Tuscany, adding to their strength, and they soon became a dangerous centre, whither some of Manfred's most faithful barons, the brothers Capece and the Lancia, after escaping from Charles's prisons, also betook themselves. Manfred was dead and his children in hopeless imprisonment, but Conradin, Frederick II.'s young grandson, and the legitimate heir of the Sicilian kingdom, was living in Germany, and the imperial eagle's nest had reared another eaglet which was pluming itself for flight. He was now about fifteen, handsome, amiable, well trained in arms, acquainted with letters and poetry, and inspired by the burning love of glory inherent in all his race. The Sicilian malcontents and exiles fixed their eyes on him, and in their own name, as also in that of the whole Ghibelline party, went to him and invited him to Italy to recover the kingdom. Pisa secretly favoured the enterprise; from all parts the Ghibellines made him offers of troops and money; the Saracens of Lucera, the southern provinces, and Sicily were exasperated by the Angevin oppression, and only waited for his coming to rise. It seemed as if his grandfather, Frederick II., had had greater obstacles to contend with when he had left Sicily to reconquer the German crown, and now before him the path lay inverted. Conradin consented to follow it, and once more a Suabian looked down from the Alps with his gaze fixed on the farthest shores of the Italian sea.

Italy was deeply moved by the news of these preparations, party passions flared up afresh, and the Pope felt with grief that a struggle which he had thought at an end was again beginning. He did all he could to calm the rising tempest, but without success. The position of the Guelphs in Tuscany grew more and more serious, and Pisa and Siena were already in arms against them, with many of Manfred's German soldiers in their pay. The Pope, alarmed at seeing the Guelphs unable to oppose the advancing wave, asked Charles to provide for the emergency, thus exactly though unwillingly meeting the wishes of the ambitious monarch, for whom a successful move in Tuscany might have all the same significance that the battle of Montaperti had once had for Manfred. Charles immediately sent eight hundred knights under Guy of Monfort, who entered Florence on Easter day 1267. Soon afterwards, as things continued to grow worse, Clement allowed Charles to go in person to Tuscany with the title of Peacemaker, in order to reduce that province to order while the imperial throne was vacant, but he was not under any circumstances to retain that post for more than three years. Charles soon went to Florence, which elected him podestà for ten years, and at the head of the Guelphs whom he collected round him he began a pitiless war against the Ghibellines, without paying any attention to the Pope's remonstrances and entreaties that he should moderate his instinctive cruelty. The exasperated Ghibellines redoubled their opposition and their hatred, and urged Conradin to hasten his approach.

The young prince responded readily. In vain the Pope threatened him with excommunication and violently denounced the young serpent, issue of the cobra, who with his breath was poisoning Tuscany; Conradin received assistance, collected followers, and announced his coming to the Italians. While he was preparing for the expedition his partisans were not idle. Conrad Capece, appointed vicar royal in Sicily, went with Pisan ships to Tunis, where he found Frederick of Castile, brother of the senator of Rome, and persuaded him to join in an attempt on Sicily. They landed there with only a few hundred soldiers and found people inclined to the revolt, which rapidly spread through the greater part of the island, and even reached the mainland. At the same time Conradin left Germany followed by a tolerably numerous army and by several barons, among whom was Rudolf of Hapsburg, on whose head the imperial crown was later destined to rest, and the young Duke of Austria, Frederick of Baden, Conradin's cousin and friend from childhood, and, like himself, disinherited, who came with him to share his fortunes faithfully till death.

Conradin reached Verona with his followers on the 20th of October 1267, and was received joyfully by the Ghibellines. A few days before Galvano Lancia, preceding him, had arrived in Rome, where the senator, Henry of Castile, received him with great honour, and having had the alliance of Conradin with the Romans proclaimed in the Capitol, did all he could to forward the cause of his ally. The nobility who were opposed to him were either imprisoned or obliged to fly, and for the assistance of Conradin, who was without money, not only was their confiscated property used, but Henry audaciously laid hands on the deposits intrusted to the churches and on Church treasures. The Roman priests complained of the sacrilege, and the Pope bewailed it from Viterbo, but did not venture to put Rome under an interdict, as he still hoped to detach Henry from an alliance likely to prove fatal to the Church. Instead of that, the anathema fell on Conradin's young head. He was still at Verona, and in the January of 1268 moved on to Pavia, the reason of his slow progress being the scarcity of means, so that if Charles of Anjou had been able to meet him in Lombardy without loss of time, the war might perhaps have been finished at a single blow. But Charles also had obstacles to contend with. The Pope hindered him, the Tuscan Ghibellines grew more and more threatening, and in his kingdom the rebellion was taking alarming proportions, especially after the Saracens of Lucera had raised on their walls the imperial standard of the Hohenstaufen and were prepared to defend it in arms. Charles, after some fighting in Tuscany, recognised the necessity of returning to his kingdom and putting down the revolts there, while he waited for his rival to reach him, unless first stopped by the Guelphs in Lombardy or Tuscany. He did this, but left a stout body of troops behind in Tuscany under the orders of his marshal, and on his journey south had an interview with the Pope, who solemnly repeated the sentence of excommunication against Conradin. This time also the senator, Henry of Castile, and the magistrates of the Capitol were included in it, only to Henry was granted a month in which to make amends. If after that term he had done nothing, then Charles was empowered to resume the senatorial dignity for ten years, " so that he may govern the city peacefully, and that we and our brethren, who could not yet visit it, may have free access to it."

While Charles was preparing to defend his kingdom, and, with the object of suppressing the revolt, was laying siege to Lucera, Conradin had advanced from Pavia, meeting with few hindrances, and on reaching Pisa, was received with solemn forms of homage, was offered support in men, ships, and money, and grew stronger every day. Wishing to go on to Rome in order to join Henry of Castile, he resolved to go by land, and leaving Pisa on the 15th of June 1268, he marched towards Siena, while a Pisan fleet, commanded by Frederick Lancia, sailed for the Calabrian coast. Conradin met with no difficulty as far as Siena, but Charles's marshal, with his eight hundred French lances, hoped by a rapid march to turn the flank of Conradin's army in some difficult spot and stop his way. Things fell out differently, however, and he himself, surprised at Ponte a Valle on the Arno, was utterly routed and taken prisoner. After this first important feat of arms, the road to Rome remained open to Conradin, who marched past Viterbo with his soldiers under the eyes of the Pope, whose courage, nevertheless, did not give way. "We know it of certain knowledge, and you must hold it as an article of faith," prophesied the Pontiff in those days, "that this ill-starred youth is doomed to destruction ; he is dragged by wicked men as a lamb to the slaughter." Conradin, following his fate, reached Monte Mario, and Rome revealed herself to his youthful eyes in a halo of memories and hopes.

The descendant of Frederick Barbarossa came to

Rome as a friend to the Ghibelline republic, and his entry was a triumph which lasted for several days amidst feasts and rejoicings. Meanwhile the Pisan fleet had defeated in the waters of Messina Charles's admiral, Robert of Lavena, and in Sicily the revolt grew in vigour, and everything promised victory to Conradin, who, on the 18th of August 1268, left Rome at the head of his army, which had been joined by Henry of Castile and many of the Roman nobility. But Charles of Anjou, with his long experience of war, was ready then for the defence, and knew the spot where he could best dispute the path to the throne. Up to the last moment he kept near the besieged town of Lucera, to prevent the Saracens being able to leave it in order to rouse the country against him and take him in the rear; then, when he knew of Conradin's approach, he marched rapidly to meet him on the confines of the kingdom. Not far from the lake of Celano, in the valley of the Salto, the two armies met, near Tagliacozzo, which has given the name to the battle, but nearer still to the town of Scurcola. There, on the 23rd of August, the fray began, which lasted the whole day with great bloodshed, and was fought with obstinacy and valour on both sides. Victory remained long uncertain, and as the day declined it seemed to smile on Conradin. Two bands of French soldiery, one after the other, were routed and put to flight, followed furiously by the Ghibellines and Germans, who became scattered in their thirst for blood and booty. But among the dark gullies of the Marsican mountains Charles of Anjou lay hidden with a third band,

and suddenly appearing on the field, changed the destinies of the day. The victors of an hour before were in their turn hopelessly routed, and the slaughter which followed was the greatest then on record. The bloody battle of Benevento seemed in comparison to this a small matter to Charles, who on the same day wrote to the Pope amidst the corpses that were heaped around him on the field of his victory.

On that field lay the flower of all the knights who had followed Conradin from Germany and Lombardy, from Tuscany and Rome. Those who survived and were not taken prisoners fled in confusion and with little hope of safety, carried hither and thither as their fate or their despair guided them. Conradin, with Frederick of Austria, Galvano Lancia and his son, and a few other faithful adherents, retraced his steps and reached Rome, but the report of their disaster had preceded them. The names of the Roman Ghibellines who had nobly died at Tagliacozzo were already known, and Pietro di Vico, the prefect of Rome, had returned to the city mortally wounded. At the same time the Guelphs were venturing back; some of them had fought with Charles, and were able to relate the details of the great victory. To remain in Rome was evidently impossible, and Conradin with his faithful companion Frederick threw himself into the Campagna on chance, seeking refuge. They wandered for some time, then reached the seashore at Astura near the Pontine marshes, in sight of Cape Circello. There were boats on the shore, and could they get into the open and touch Sicily or reach Pisa, they would certainly be saved, and perhaps there was still hope of overcoming misfortune and changing again the decree of destiny. They embarked, but soon other ships followed and stopped them. These ships belonged to the lord of Astura, John Frangipane, whose family had long favoured the house of Suabia, and had been favoured by it. It was useless to resist, and the name gave confidence to Conradin, who surrendered, and was taken first to Astura, then to another castle farther inland. Neither prayers nor promises could induce Frangipane to set Conradin at liberty, and he only hesitated between handing him over to Charles or to the Pope, to whom for some years the Frangipane had again drawn near. An unlucky fate brought just at that moment and to that part of the coast the admiral Robert of Lavena, anxious to wipe out from Charles's memory his defeat at Messina. By threats and promises he obtained from Frangipane the custody of the royal prisoner and of his companion Frederick, and the two youths were handed over to the vengeance of the ruthless Angevin.

Nor was vengeance slow in coming, and it was inexorable and cruel. In torrents flowed the blood of the barons taken at Tagliacozzo, or seized upon here and there in their miserable wanderings; and one of the first who suffered was Manfred's uncle, Galvano Lancia, whose death was rendered more bitter by the sight of his son murdered first before his eyes. Charles betook himself to Rome to resume the senatorial dignity, then soon returned to Naples, dragging after him those prisoners who had not yet suffered death, and were awaiting their fate in the prisons of Palestrina. Among them were Conradin and Frederick of Austria, and the senator Henry of Castile. The life of this latter was spared, but he languished in prison for more than twenty years, while Conradin and Frederick were doomed to death. The Pope had no part in it, but was silent, as if unwilling to plead for mercy. The sentence was heard by the two youths with calmness, and on the 29th of October 1268 they mounted together the fatal scaffold, around which the people pressed, half in pity, half in terror. The tyrant who had condemned them was himself present, and witnessed the intrepidity with which the last of the Hohenstaufen bent his neck to the executioner, worthy of the brave race which died with him. The imagination of the pitying people surrounded with legends this fair ill-fated heir of a mysteriously tragic destiny, and later their fury avenged his death at the Sicilian Vespers. The house of Suabia was extinct, and the Church seemed to breathe more freely after a century of gigantic struggles. But new struggles were preparing, and the French influence invoked by the Popes was destined not only to turn against the Papacy, but, worse still, to humiliate it. At Palermo the vesper-bell was to sound the hour of vengeance for the blood of Manfred and Conradin; while at Anagni the men of Philip le Bel, led by Nogaret and Sciarra, in forcing themselves into the apartments of Boniface VIII., were destined to drag through the mud the Church which had invoked French intervention in Italy.

> "Veggio in Alagna entrar lo fiordaliso
> E nel vicario suo Cristo esser catto !"

INDEX.

———+·———

PRINTED BY BALLANTYNE, HANSON AND CO.
EDINBURGH AND LONDON